CREATING YOUR DREAM BATHROOM

HOW TO PLAN AND STYLE THE PERFECT SPACE

CREATING YOUR DREAM BATHROOM

HOW TO PLAN AND STYLE THE PERFECT SPACE

SUSAN BREEN

Sterling Publishing Co., Inc.

New York

This page
Art Deco hotel style is exemplified by
this stunning bathroom at an island
hotel in Devon, England.
Previous page
Floor to ceiling mirrored surfaces,
polished stone, tile, and glass are the
four natural elements used here.

Created by Lynn Bryan, The BookMaker, London.
Design by Mary Staples.
Photography by Douglas Hill.
Contributors: Lynn Bryan,
Andrew Bannister, and Jan Orchard.

Library of Congress Cataloging-in-Publication Data Available

1 2 3 4 5 6 7 8 9 10

Published by Sterling Publishing Co., Inc.
387 Park Avenue South, New York, NY 10016
© 2005 by Susan Breen
Distributed in Canada by Sterling Publishing
C/o Canadian Manda Group, 165 Dufferin Street
Toronto, Ontario, Canada M6K 3H6
Distributed in Great Britain by Chrysalis Books Group PLC
The Chrysalis Building, Bramley Road, London W10 6SP, England
Distributed in Australia by Capricorn Link (Australia) Pty. Ltd.
P.O. Box 704, Windsor, NSW 2756, Australia

Printed in China
All rights reserved

Sterling ISBN-13: 978-1-4027-2420-6
ISBN-10: 1-4027-2420-9

For information about custom editions, special sales, premium and
corporate purchases, please contact Sterling Special Sales
Department at 800-805-5489 or specialsales@sterlingpub.com.

CONTENTS

PART TWO
Case Studies 82

A DETAILED LOOK AT
A SELECTION OF PERSONAL
PAMPERING SPACES.

INTRODUCTION

The simple, functional bathroom of a decade ago has become a retreat where you can indulge the senses. Dimmed lights or chic candles emitting a relaxing aroma, bubbles swirling in the tub, and a locked door result in a totally relaxing mood. As a stress-buster, there is no better place than the bathroom.

The change in our attitude to the bathroom probably began with the desire to separate the adult bathroom from that of the children. Too many outraged parents have been kept waiting outside the bathroom door while family members refused to come out until they were ready. This scenario led to two- (or more) bathroom homes becoming the norm. Now the challenge is to make these more than physical cleansing spaces—the influences of both hotel bathroom design and spa resort bathrooms are reflected in the desire for a chill-out zone at home.

Above
A custom shelf within the cabinet unit was designed to hold towels.

Opposite
Dark wood makes an impact in this large bathroom. Natural flooring tile completes the design.

Bathrooms are the talk of the home improvement business, overtaking the demand for new kitchens. In new homes or remodeling projects, the transformation can be dramatic. The bathroom is now regarded as the starting point for a home, rather than as just another space within an architect's scheme.

There are luxurious bathtubs, showers, saunas, and steam rooms designed for the home spa, manufactured for all budgets. Water no longer just trickles out of the showerhead or the faucet. It flows, streams, and/or pulsates with soothing power over the body.

Another prominent trend is the idea of an all-in-one sleeping and bathing space, often with a dressing room, too. Designers also use the term "wet and dry rooms" in the context of the modern bathroom. Wet areas include steam, showers, saunas, and deep

soaking tubs. Shower stalls have become sculptural spaces, more like indoor fountains of health-giving pleasure. Dry areas include space for aerobics, stretching, riding an exercise cycle, and yoga. You might also find a refrigerator and a space where you can blend fresh fruit juice, or make early morning hot beverages.

In the bathroom, attention to detail matters more than in any other room. A vanity is now the focal point, designed with a right-sized area for everything from a hair dryer to makeup. Technology has also moved media into the bathroom. You can watch television while in the bathtub on a screen that slides away when you are done, mirrors never mist up, music is piped into the shower unit, and the Internet can be accessed while you dress.

This beautifully photographed book looks at the options you face as you consider renovating an existing, or creating a new, bathroom. It is divided into two sections. The first examines the practical options, asks you to assess which features you want in your dream bathroom, and gives advice on planning, space solutions, ventilation, and achieving a unique style. Details of the types of materials for surfaces such as walls, floors, and ceilings are presented, followed by a feature on tile. The vanity unit and the countertop, types of cabinetry, storage, and a look at hardware follow. Appropriate lighting and a chapter on fixtures and accessories bring the first section to a close.

New and remodeled bathrooms in private homes are featured in the second part of the book. Superb color photographs present fabulous new ideas and the accompanying text talks about the process of designing these bathrooms.

Here, you will find inspiration and practical ideas to help you design a bathroom to make bathing at home even more pleasurable.

Above
An elegant glass vase and blue iris flowers bring the colors in the mosaic tile on the countertop to life.

Opposite
Mosaic tile enlivens this renovated bathroom.

PART ONE

FUNCTION AND DESIGN

PRACTICALS

Function is how the bathroom and its components perform their tasks. Design is how you achieve that and how it eventually looks. In the following pages we look at how to plan for both characteristics in your new and unique bathroom.

DETERMINE YOUR NEEDS

Selecting the functions of a bathroom is the first important step in the creation of a new bathroom. Unless you have a clear idea of what you want you will find it challenging to accomplish your task.

Since the main function of a bathroom is to cleanse the body, the first issue to discuss is how you want to do this. Do you want a bathtub, a shower, or both? Do you want one or two sinks? Have you a preference for separate hot and cold faucets or do you like a mixer faucet? There are good arguments for all of the previous, but in the end it comes down to personal preference. And that means speaking to all family members who might use the bathroom, and listening to their needs. Then you can make a list of everything practical required for your dream design.

Every item you place on your list will have a function that requires careful consideration in the planning stage of the new bathroom.

Since a bathtub is the largest item, think about how many times you or your family will use it. If you like a soak at the end of a stressful day, then a soaking tub is the one for you. However, does this suit the other people who use the bathroom? Do you have room for both a soaking tub and a shower? The size of the basic tub you select will have an effect on how many other items on the list

- ▶ **Bathtub**
- ▶ **Sink**
- ▶ **Large separate shower**
- ▶ **Shower over the tub**
- ▶ **Flooring**
- ▶ **Toilet**
- ▶ **Bidet**
- ▶ **Vanity unit**
- ▶ **Free-standing storage units**
- ▶ **Open shelves**
- ▶ **Illuminated mirrors**
- ▶ **Shaving and beauty mirrors**
- ▶ **Light fixtures for ceiling, walls, and special vanity fixtures**
- ▶ **Ventilation that turns on when you come into the room**
- ▶ **Towel warmers**
- ▶ **Matching hardware**
- ▶ **Electrical outlets**

PLUS A WISH LIST WHICH MIGHT INCLUDE

- ▶ **Underfloor heating**
- ▶ **Waterfall shower**
- ▶ **Color-changing lighting**
- ▶ **Integrated music system**
- ▶ **Media (television or computer)**
- ▶ **Soaking tub**
- ▶ **Whirlpool**
- ▶ **Steam room**
- ▶ **Plunge pool**

you can fit into an average bathroom. If you select a waterfall shower, remember that both a large tub and a waterfall shower require a lot of hot water so you might have to replace your existing water tank. You will need to budget for that cost.

Choosing a toilet suite and a sink are also major decisions *(see pages 74–75 and 80),* as is the selection of the vanity unit and storage facilities. Remember that moving the plumbing will cost quite a bit of money, so try to work with what is already in place.

The amount of natural light that the bathroom gets throughout the day will determine the amount of artificial lighting you will need. The decisions on electrical outlets and light and ventilation fittings must be made at the planning stage. It is too expensive to add electrical outlets and light sockets during the actual building stage.

Flooring is probably the next major decision *(see Flooring, page 36),* followed by the type of wall surface *(see Wall, page 32).* Once you have these details in place, you can think about the type and style of light fixtures, whether you want an entire wall of mirror or just a few well-placed, wall-hung mirrors, elaborate towel warmers, and any other of the wish-list items.

By now you are well on the way to a finished list of bathroom requirements. Now you need to do the budget.

Right

The owners of this beach house wanted a sitting area adjacent the ensuite so they could see the sea.

BUDGET

Creating a budget for work to be done in the bathroom is easier than you might think. The key to budgeting is to follow these simple rules. First, you need to understand that a bathroom consists of two areas of cost, the supplies and the installations.

SUPPLIES

List every item you have decided you want to include in your new bathroom. As you selected your products you would have noted prices. Some supplies, such as basic pipe work, will be included in the installer price. However, you should establish this at the start to ensure you are not surprised later on.

INSTALLATIONS

The cost of installations will depend on how complicated your current or new bathroom layout is (is the room an odd shape, are there difficult corners or varying floor levels, etc). How you want it finished comes into this cost equation, too. Installers will require detailed plans on how the room is to be finished, so preparation of the plans and the accompanying details is very important to ensure that you get as accurate as possible prices from the plumbers, carpenters, electricians, tilers, and painters who will work on your project. Make sure you have covered everything that needs to be installed, starting from the ceiling and working down to the floor.

Once you have a price for both the supplies and the installation you will soon discover if everything you desire is affordable or not. This is the point when you may have to start deleting wish-list items from the budget.

You must also remember to keep an amount to one side for the unforeseen. Professionals would suggest you keep at least ten percent of the total budget to one side and tell no one. This is your reserve fund for any problems that may require attention, such as the dry wall and framing need extending a little further than was first estimated; the hot and cold supplies coming into the bathroom turn out to be inadequate, and perhaps the unstable floor requires additional support. None of these things could have been foreseen and they all cost money.

The amount of money you have to spend will drive the bathroom. A large budget will allow you freedom of product choice; and a low, but reasonable, budget might restrict your selection of products. More often than not, you will discover that the installation cost is higher than first anticipated, which can lead to a rethink on product selection.

So if this is the first time you have

reach. How close are the sinks to the window, and is the toilet too close to the door? The last thing you want to see as you enter the room is the toilet, so try to place the sink(s) and vanity unit in view rather than less attractive items.

Also, consider where the vanity is to be located and, if you want to sit down in front of the mirror, make sure there is enough space for a small chair or vanity stool, plus space for another person to pass by while you are seated there.

Wet rooms are now becoming the standard in modern bathrooms. A wet room is an area, or a complete room, where the shower requires no shower tray. Instead, the water runs away through a specially constructed floor and drainage system. You do not require a shower screen to prevent the stream of water from splashing.

However, you must ensure that the installers are competent in everything they do, creating a completely watertight seal on all surfaces to prevent leakages. A last point to consider: If you are considering a wet room, make sure you position a wood vanity or any other wood cabinetry away from water spray to avoid damaging the unit.

UNIVERSAL DESIGN ADVANTAGES

A well-designed bathroom will provide a lifetime of comfort and relaxation. One of the best ways to accomplish this is to incorporate what are known as Universal Design features during the initial design phase. Simply stated, the goal of Universal Design is to create safe spaces accessible to every member of the family regardless of age, size, or physical ability. In other words, a bathroom designed today should accommodate everybody throughout each stage of life.

For example, adding a 15-inch ledge to one end of a bathtub creates a convenient place to store soaps, towels, and bath oils, but may also be used as a seated transition area to assist an elderly, or injured, member of the family getting in and out of the tub. Similarly, selecting a handheld shower, rather than a fixed unit, adds the flexibility to adjust the spray to suit different family members, makes it easier to assist a young child, or to clean the shower. Installing bathroom faucets and handles on the side of the bathtub, rather than in the middle, places the fixtures within reach and eliminates a person's having to bend when filling the bathtub.

Evaluate your bathroom to see where you might benefit from adding Universal Design features. The first aspect to consider is the size of the room. When it comes to Universal Design, bigger is always better. A larger room translates to more space to move about comfortably or assist a family member who may need help from time to time. On average, the typical residential bathroom is a mere 5 x 7 feet.

If you are remodeling a small-sized bathroom, consider borrowing space from

Opposite

Storage units with many levels are ideal for a family where members might range in age from very young to old. Here there is a space for each to reach.

surrounding rooms or closets, or bumping out an exterior wall to enlarge the bathroom. If you are designing a new bathroom, keep in mind that, at a minimum, the space should be large enough for two people to comfortably share the grooming area and to incorporate a separate toilet area for privacy as well.

Since more fall-related injuries take place in the bathroom than in any other room in the home, take particular care when choosing the flooring. Look at the qualities of resilient, low- maintenance, slip-resistant surfaces that reduce the chances of a fall, particularly when the surface is wet. Matte-finish ceramic tile, tumbled stone, and embossed vinyl all offer nonslip surfaces that provide traction. If choosing wood flooring, be sure to finish the surface with a nonskid penetrating sealer.

When bathroom plans call for two sinks, lower one of them from the standard 36 inches off the floor down to 30 inches to make that fixture more accessible for a very young child or a seated person.

Similarly, choosing well-designed and strong single-lever sink, tub, and shower faucets is an unobtrusive way to add ease of use without compromising the style of the rest of the bathroom.

Safety grab bars, once considered an institutional-looking bathroom feature, are now manufactured in a wide assortment of styles that coordinate with other bathroom fittings. In fact, the latest reinforced grab bars look much like smart towel bars. For stability, grab bars must be installed in the wall studs during construction and be able to support a minimum of 200 pounds.

STEPS FOR A SAFER BATHROOM

▶ OPT FOR ROUNDED, RATHER THAN SQUARED, VANITY EDGES TO PREVENT INJURES THAT CAN RESULT WHEN YOU BUMP INTO SHARP CORNERS.

▶ ADD AN ILLUMINATED LIGHT SWITCH ON THE WALL JUST OUTSIDE THE BATHROOM TO SAFELY LIGHT THE WAY INTO THE ROOM AT NIGHT.

▶ LOWER LIGHT SWITCHES A FEW INCHES TO PLACE THEM WITHIN REACH OF YOUNG CHILDREN.

▶ TILTING VANITY MIRRORS MOUNTED ON SWIVELS CAN ACCOMMODATE FAMILY MEMBERS OF ALL HEIGHTS.

▶ A SHOULDER-LEVEL RECESSED NICHE BUILT INTO THE SHOWER WALL ELIMINATES THE NEED TO BEND OVER TO REACH SOAPS AND SHAMPOOS.

TO LEARN MORE ABOUT UNIVERSAL DESIGN, AND TO LOCATE AN EXPERIENCED PROFESSIONAL IN YOUR AREA, VISIT THE NATIONAL KITCHEN AND BATHROOM ASSOCIATION'S WEBSITE AT WWW.NKBA.COM OR LOCATE AN ARCHITECT WHO SPECIALIZES IN THIS AREA OF DESIGN.

VENTILATION

In today's energy-efficient homes, the extra layers of insulation and tight construction that keep the home warm in the winter and cool in the summer are the same factors that create the potential for mold, mildew, and poor air quality. In locations like the kitchen and bathroom, where constant exposure to moisture creates high humidity, good ventilation is essential to the long-term health of the home and the people who live in it.

Domestic condensation is a nuisance. Cloudy water droplets form on windows,

metal window frames, bathroom tiles, mirrors, and stainless steel equipment. Condensation occurs when rising hot air comes into contact with a cold surface. The result is condensation because the moisture vapor condenses back into tiny opaque droplets of water. (The exact temperature at which this happens is called the dew point.)

The most desirable form of ventilation in the bathroom is an open window that naturally replenishes fresh air and can quickly reduce moisture content. However, interior rooms and those bathrooms with large showers with multiple sprays, or whirlpool tubs that kick up a cloud of steam, will need a more efficient means of venting moisture to the outside of the home. In many parts of the country, local codes define the type and amount of ventilation necessary to meet building standards. For this reason, home owners should check regulations to guarantee compliance before installing a ventilation system.

A well-designed bathroom fan will shift the entire volume of air at least four to five times an hour. This will not work unless the bathroom door has a gap underneath or a louver in it to allow the air to flow through. Clean the fan and the filter regularly.

Ceiling-mounted ventilation fans are rated by the volume of air they circulate per minute. Fans are designed to move from 70 to 600 cfm's (cubic feet per minute). The average bathroom with a combination tub and shower unit will generally require a fan with a 70 cfm rating. In a large bathroom, with several different moisture-generating fixtures, each area should have its own ventilation unit.

Above
Locating the tub near a window that can open to let steam out is the ideal situation in a bathroom.

New fans are designed to be less conspicuous by combining ventilation with a recessed light fixture for a less cluttered look on the ceiling. Other new introductions feature fans with preprogrammed sensors that automatically cycle the unit on when the room's humidity reaches a certain level.

In addition to cfm measurement home owners should pay attention to the amount of noise generated by ventilation fans. In the past, larger motors meant higher noise levels. Increasingly, more powerful (as well as more expensive) fans feature whisper-quiet operation, with barely discernable noise levels.

When shopping, note that fan noise is rated by sones; the lower the sone rating, the quieter the fan. In large master suites made up of many small-sized rooms, another option is to install an air duct system. This type of bath ventilation involves a network of fans vented through a duct system that leads to a motor located in a remote part of the home. The motor pulls the moist air out of the room and vents it to the outdoors. Though air duct systems are the most complex style of ventilation, they are also the most efficient. They are also the quietest method of ventilation because the remote location of the motor guarantees a virtually silent operation in the bathroom.

Left
This shower is set outside of the home and needs no ventilation. The floor area around it is pebbled to prevent anyone's slipping on a wet surface.

SETTING THE STYLE

Once little more than a small room with a utilitarian vanity and mirror (showing only the top half of the body), the bathroom has become the center of personal grooming.

Personal space is a priority in a bathroom that is bigger and open plan in design than it was a few years ago. The challenge in creating a successful bathing zone is to harmonize the area's style to the master suite, while retaining the idea of its being separate space.

Selecting a style for your bathroom depends upon many factors. Ideally, the area should reflect the decorating style of the adjacent master bedroom. If you are decorating a family/guest bathroom, the design should reflect the style of the home, with a few personal finishing touches. If you live in a Period home (for example, Victorian, American Colonial, or Art Deco), the bathroom could be designed in the same style. However, you might want a surprise as you walk into the room and that calls for something completely different.

Finding a style that suits your personality and the established décor of your home is the first step in establishing a design to adhere to as you begin the process of selecting a tub, shower unit, and the other products necessary to complete your dream bathroom. This will ensure all of the fixtures and accessories are of a similar style, and that you do not mix period pieces or styles.

The first thing to do is to close your mind to outside influences and suggestions. This is your bathroom, so let it be your style

Left

This is great styling. The accessories and the faucet are similar in feel to the wrought-iron vanity, as is the wall sconce. The sink color is similar to the paintwork's.

and not someone else's. What you need is a starting point, which could be a favorite color, the pattern of a wallpaper, or a bathroom item you may have already selected, and which suggests a specific theme. It's worth remembering that some materials immediately conjure up certain responses.

For instance, dark wood paneling evokes masculinity; marble of any color is elegance personified; rough-hewn tiles are definitely Mediterranean; chrome and sandblasted opaque glass are modern, as is limestone tile (despite the fact it is a traditional material). Walls inset with a border of patterned tiles might indicate that a traditionalist bathes here, as could a black and white tile floor.

Once you have determined a style, focus on it. If you live in a home with no specific style, and no strong color scheme, look around the bathroom area. Is it dark or light? Are you looking to create a colorful room (bright pink in the early morning?), or a relaxing environment (cool pale blue hues work well)? Do you like natural stone materials in a classic setting, or do you feel more at home with modern steel and glass? Fond of ornate style, where carved corbels and gilded mirrors combine with fancy gold-plated faucets and polished marble tiling? Or is minimalism your look?

A study of design magazines and books will give you an idea of current styles. Photocopy the designs that interest you and create a design file or tear sheets. You can share these ideas with other members of the family, and a design consultant if you decide to go with a bathroom company.

Whatever your personal style, it is good to remember that the bathroom is the first place you visit in the morning, therefore its decoration needs to be practical as well as imaginative. Faucets should let water flow strongly; a shower area needs to be easy to enter and leave; towel bars should be useful. An item that is divinely stylish but impractical will frustrate you and the family.

Below

Shabui slate floor tiles and rustic gold slate wall tiles combine with a single sheet of floating tempered glass screen in this shower unit.

THE POWDER ROOM

Here is a space where your design can be fun or serious, fancy or minimalist, bright or subtle. It's the showcase of your personal style.

mirrors on all the walls and the ceiling, display children's artwork, display grown-up artwork, or leave the entire space white.

Full-on gilded mirror frames set above a decorated sink and expensive wallpaper set above a dado rail, lit by a crystal chandelier, will make a statement firmly placing you as a successful traditionalist with a flair for the dramatic. Or perhaps your style is more of a minimal look mirroring your clean-cut professional personality. A sleek Oriental-style black-stained vanity unit accented by a frosted-glass sink, with discreet drawers that open at a touch, set against a red lacquered wall, will create a contrasting effect.

This is one place where guests get to visit and it can become the talking point of any social occasion. It's a space where guests can privately admire your style, or not! There are some basic design rules to apply: Large patterns can overwhelm a small space; bright colors can be a little garish. Pale colors will make the room seem larger, and dark colors will enclose the space. White will make the ceiling seem higher than it is; dark color will bring it down. One of the best things about your powder room is the cost to make it impressive. For a reasonable cost, you can transform it into a thing of beauty.

The key to this small and private place is imagination, using color, materials with texture, and paint or wallpaper (good for this room because there is no fear of steam or

Above

A custom sink shines with a silk pomegranate design wallcovering in a gabardine hue. Sea green stone and a matte platinum faucet finish it off.

To an interior designer with a playful soul, this room is the single most popular room where you can experiment, even be outrageous, with your design ideas. This small sanctuary can be as personal as you want it to be. Anything goes in this space. You can cram its walls with framed family snapshots, add pink lace frills around the mirror, paint gold leaf in patterns across the ceiling and walls, use water damage), or both. Choose a flooring that's smooth, durable, and easy to maintain. Avoid using carpet in this area. Fittings such as sinks and faucets should make a design statement in keeping with the rest of the style. Here is the ideal home for gold taps if you are so inclined, or flights of fancy.

Existing fittings do not need to be changed if the budget is low. It is important to hide all pipe work as this is unattractive to the eye (unless of course it is a design feature within the cutting-edge theme of the room). Instead of shifting the toilet to a new position, you could hide the cistern by building a box around it, from the floor up, and capping the top of the boxed area with a layer of natural stone.

Make sure there is enough room between an open door and the toilet. Being cramped is not an option for your guests in this situation!

If the room has just one small radiator, perhaps change it for a smart towel warmer to match the period of your design.

One way of making the space feel bigger is to use mirrors, on all surfaces if you so desire, or mirror one entire side wall and place the vanity on the other so you have an uninterrupted reflection. For an interesting effect, make the entire ceiling a light box that changes color throughout the day and night.

A powder room requires excellent ventilation, especially if it is entirely enclosed. Guests walking into a clean and fresh-smelling environment will notice the difference. Air needs to be changed regularly and perhaps scented at the same time. The best type of extraction is where air passes out

through the ceiling, this being the highest point in a room. Alternatively, air can be vented through the wall. *(See Ventilation, page 24.)*

Motion detectors that will turn on venters when you walk into the room or timers can be purchased within lighting switchs. They are inexpensive, but must be installed by a qualified electrician.

Key lighting is another important design element in a powder room. Lighting can be used to great effect. You can use a single spotlight set in the ceiling to shine down onto a sink, a painting, or a small tableau on the countertop. Or you could use a light fixture set into the floor that will shine up a wall, making the wall a focal point. Bouncing light off a wall with uplighters is also effective.

Above

Chandeliers and mirrors have created an adorable exotic powder room.

SURFACES

Whether you prefer shimmering glass tiles, a smooth solid surface, textured hardwoods, or the latest laminates, you will find information to help you select surface materials to set the style of the bathroom without compromising the concepts of durability and low maintenance.

WALL STYLE

Bathroom walls represent the largest decorative surface, and are perhaps the greatest design opportunity in the room. Less wear and tear on walls means more flexibility when it comes to expressing your style.

Wall treatments will need to withstand exposure to moisture and steam, but beyond that, there is no limit to your design creativity. To begin the process, imagine the room as an empty space with just the four walls, windows, and a door. Then consider the size and layout of the room. Both of these factors will determine the design direction for the walls.

There are many design ideas to choose from. If you want the walls to blend into the background, it is best to use neutral colors to complement both the countertops and the flooring.

Deep, saturated hues will create a sensation in smaller spaces; however, it is best not to create an overpowering feeling with too much color. In a large space, color can define spaces.

Installing an entire wall of mirror from floor to ceiling in a lackluster space will build drama by adding depth to the room. Or, you may choose to completely change the existing character of the bathroom with a few coats of a textured-finish paint.

Wall applications can also reinforce the style of your space. For example, a large expanse of white ceramic subway tile punctuated with a line of tuxedo trim gives off the glamour of the 1930s.

Look around your immediate environment for inspiration. An exterior-facing wall lined with smooth river rock will connect the master bathroom of a mountain retreat with terrain just outside the door (in addition to adding a layer of natural insulation to maintain an even temperature year round). If you love that old-fashioned country style, beaded board panels will generate a farmhouse feel while crisp, white moldings and trim will suggest the elegance of a Grand Hotel belonging to a bygone era.

On the following pages are some decorative starter points for you to consider.

Left
In a guest bathroom, painted wood panel insets create an interesting wall surface.

Opposite
Wide old wood floor planks, a cathedral-like ceiling, and white paintwork on doors that open onto a deck all combine to make this traditional bath by the beach simply appealing.

COLOR

Nothing wakes up weary walls faster than color. Paint, the most popular wall treatment in the bathroom, is an affordable design option that allows you to experiment without making a large investment of time or money. Neutral shades create a quiet mood while bold wall color infuses the space with energy. Match wall color to materials found elsewhere in the bathroom. It is a good idea to test two or three tones of the color you like by painting each onto a small section of wall to observe how various shades react in different types of light. Choose washable acrylic paints in satin or gloss finishes that are mildew resistant and easy to clean.

MIRRORS

Visually expand the height, width, and depth of your bathroom with the use of wall mirrors. Large mirrored panels work wonders to reflect natural and artificial light, or bring a beautiful outdoor view into the room. Since light levels differ dramatically throughout the day, experiment by placing a small mirror on a section of wall for a few days to get a better understanding of how a mirror will have an impact on the space. As an example, placing a large mirror opposite a window will amplify daylight, but may also create a blinding glare during certain times of the day. If you plan to invest in a wall-sized mirror, hire an experienced glazer to do the measuring and installation. Mirrors are costly and fragile; in the end, you will save money and time by hiring a professional.

STENCILS

Today's stencils are available as intricate designs and elaborate overlays that produce detailed murals and sophisticated *trompe l'oeil* treatments in the bathroom. Overall patterns create the illusion of handpainted or mosaic tile with realistic results, and more elaborate mural stencil sets depict scenes such as the golden hills of Tuscany, or a soothing seaside setting. Many stencil manufacturers, at a prequoted cost, can create a custom template to match a design in a fabric or a design motif that has been used as a decorative element elsewhere in the bathroom.

Above
A backsplash made of shells is the finishing touch to a wall hung with decorative mirrors of differents shapes and sizes.

Opposite
A decorative painted ceiling adds character to a room.

TEXTURE

Decorative paint-on finishes are the latest trend in bathroom wall treatments. Sold in kits at home improvement centers, they contain everything that the homeowner needs to create the look of expensive, hand-applied faux finishes at a fraction of the cost. Kits are available in a range of choices that include antique glazes, metallic looks, aged Venetian plaster, and sandy textured walls. Most may be brushed or rolled onto white or tinted walls in an easy process that involves one or two simple steps. This decorative craft can usually be completed in a weekend.

WALLPAPER

How much moisture and steam your bathing choices create is a factor to consider when choosing wallpaper for the bathroom. Sturdy, vinyl-coated or washable papers that are less susceptible to water damage are the most long-wearing and, therefore, the best choice in the bathroom. Large fixtures and unusual room configurations mean that wallpapering a bathroom can be a challenge to an inexperienced person; to ensure that corners and seams are expertly sealed and guarantee the best results, pay attention to these details, measuring them carefully before cutting the paper. Or, splurge on the services of a professional paper hanger.

THE CEILING

OFTEN REFERRED TO AS "THE FIFTH WALL," THE CEILING IS AN OFTEN OVERLOOKED DESIGN OPPORTUNITY. ONE OF THE MOST SIGNIFICANT SHIFTS IN RESIDENTIAL ARCHITECTURE HAS BEEN TO INCREASE A ROOM'S VOLUME BY RAISING THE CEILING. IN HOMES WHERE SPACE LIMITATIONS PREVENT AN INCREASE IN THE SQUARE FOOTAGE OF A BATHROOM, ADDING HEIGHT AND NATURAL LIGHT TO A ROOM CAN CREATE THE ILLUSION OF A LARGER, MORE DRAMATIC SPACE.

► CHECK YOUR HOME'S ARCHITECTURAL STRUCTURE; INCREASING VOLUME MAY BE AS SIMPLE AS ELIMINATING A DROPPED CEILING TO UNCOVER EXPOSED BEAMS, PLANKS, OR TRUSSES THAT ADD HEIGHT AND CHARACTER.

► IF RAISING THE CEILING IS NOT AN OPTION, INCREASE THE AMOUNT OF NATURAL LIGHT THROUGH A SKYLIGHT OR ROW OF CLERESTORY WINDOWS PLACED JUST BELOW THE CEILING LINE.

► CREATE THE ILLUSION OF A HIGHER CEILING BY PAINTING THE SURFACE ONE OR TWO TONES LIGHTER THAN THE WALLS AND PLACING SOFT LIGHTING IN THE CORNERS OF THE ROOM TO DRAW THE EYE UPWARD.

FLOOR STYLE

Choosing flooring for a bathroom often means walking a
fine line between the form and function of the space. The
floor represents an opportunity to create an impression of
the room's architectural style.

Left
The ultimate wet
room: floor-to-ceiling
glass walls and a
large, smooth flooring
tile combine to make
the most of the
natural beauty in this
island home.

Given the above, the material must be
durable enough to take a pounding from
heavy foot traffic as well as daily exposure to
moisture. In addition, the bathroom floor
should be easy to clean. With so much to
consider, it makes sense to research and
weigh each of the available flooring options
before finalizing the selection.

Use the style of the bathroom as a
starting point to narrow the flooring choices.
As one of the most dominant design elements
within the room, the floor must work with
other components to express the overall
aesthetic. For example, wide oak planks
paired with an antique clawfoot tub
references early 20th-century style, while a
sleek, slate floor beneath polished granite

countertops suggests an Asian-inspired, contemporary look. Crisp Carrera marble floor tile mixed with mahogany cabinets crafts a classic, timeless look, and repeating the same subtly textured stone surface on the walls and floor creates a soothing sanctuary that makes for a restful and relaxing retreat.

The function of the bathroom should also serve to guide the selection of materials. In large, open master bathrooms with distinct zones for bathing, grooming, and relaxing, many interior designers use a change of flooring to delineate the function areas of each of the spaces. You might consider terra-cotta–colored porcelain tile in the central part of the bathroom with sections of tumbled limestone for the shower and tub area. Both hues are harmonious, and they will provide a useful contrast, delineating the areas well.

Also look to adjoining rooms. When the bathroom is connected to a sleeping area or a sitting room, using the same type of flooring creates a streamlined look, and provides a smooth transition between the two spaces. This works well in small spaces, too.

Finally, allow the bathroom budget to steer you toward affordable choices in flooring. Use accurate room measurements to gather quotes on materials costs and labor estimates and be sure to have drawings in hand to show placement of large fixtures such as the bathtub, vanity, and shower.

A footnote to those with small-sized bathrooms: Limited square footage works to your advantage when in comes to choosing your dream material. Pricier floor treatments such as stone can work out to be surprisingly affordable in a petite retreat.

RADIANT HEAT

IF STEPPING ONTO A COLD TILE SURFACE FIRST THING ON A CHILLY MORNING IS NOT YOUR IDEA OF A WELCOMING WAKE-UP, CONSIDER A RADIANT HEAT SYSTEM FOR THE FLOOR. INSTALLED BETWEEN THE TILE AND SUBFLOOR, RADIANT HEAT COMES IN TWO FORMS: HYDRONIC SYSTEMS THAT USE HOT WATER AS A HEAT SOURCE AND THIN ELECTRIC PADS THAT BLANKET THE FLOOR WITH WARMTH. BOTH SYSTEMS ARE CONTROLLED BY ENERGY-EFFICIENT THERMOSTATS SET TO PREPROGRAMMED SETTINGS THAT CAN CYCLE ON AND OFF THROUGHOUT THE DAY. TIME THE HEAT TO TURN ON AN HOUR BEFORE YOU RISE SO YOUR FEET WILL GET A TREAT OF TOAST-LEVEL WARMTH, AND THEN SET IT TO SHUT OFF LATER IN THE MORNING AFTER YOU HAVE LEFT HOME FOR THE DAY.

RADIANT HEAT SYSTEMS ARE AVAILABLE THROUGH FLOORING CONTRACTORS AND TILE SHOWROOMS. THOUGH COST VARIES ACCORDING TO SQUARE FOOTAGE YOU CAN EXPECT TO PAY ABOUT $1000 TO OUTFIT AN AVERAGE 5-BY-7-FOOT BATH.

FLOORING CHOICES

Above

Wide planks have been left pale in this modern bathroom space. The wood cradle for the bath is an interesting design feature.

HARDWOOD

Pros: Wood, once considered impractical in the bathroom because of its susceptibility to water damage, is now widely used thanks to the latest generation of polyurethane sealants that shield the material from moisture. Wood is milled in an assortment of tones, grain patterns, and plank widths. Its natural beauty creates a warm contrast with cold materials such as tile, stone, and metal. Wood floors may be sealed on site or installed in prefinished planks.

Cons: The longevity of wood is determined by the quality of sealer used. If the surface is compromised, moisture seepage may cause warping and rot. Hardwood surfaces require periodic sanding and resealing to keep up a good appearance and can show signs of wear in high-traffic areas such as doorways and sink fronts.

VINYL

Pros: Vinyl is a soft, cushioned surface that makes an affordable and versatile flooring option. Sold in smooth or textured sheets and tiles in a broad range of colors and patterns, vinyl can be installed in less than a day and requires minimal subfloor preparation. In remodeled baths, vinyl can often be laid on top of existing flooring.

Cons: Vinyl scratches easily and is more prone to damage than other types of bath flooring. In the case of sheet vinyl, once damage occurs, the surface often requires replacement, rather than repair. Sunlight and harsh cleaners can dull the factory finish and cause fading over time.

LAMINATE

Pros: Laminate offers durability and easy maintenance, and is made up of a solid core beneath a realistic photograph of wood or stone, and topped with a strong, clear plastic layer. Though laminate looks natural, it is the same man-made material that is used on countertops. It cleans up with soap and water and retains its excellent appearance even in high traffic areas.

Cons: Though laminate is bathroom approved, long-term exposure to leaks or standing water will cause warping if moisture seeps beneath the top layer of the material. As an engineered product, laminate lacks the

authentic character of natural materials such as hardwood and stone. In addition, depending upon the depth and thickness of the subfloor, laminate floors can sound hollow when walked upon.

TILE

Pros: Tile offers more design flexibility than any other bath flooring option. Relatively easy to install and available in an endless array of shapes, sizes, colors, and styles, tile is easy to customize to any number of design applications. Waterproof and long-wearing, properly maintained tile floors will survive heavy wear and tear.

Cons: Since tile is slippery when wet, your safety is a big consideration when installing smooth-surfaced tile in a bathroom. For that reason, only low-sheen, skid-resistant tile approved for use as flooring should be considered; when in doubt, consult a flooring contractor. Grout lines require periodic sealing and add to the high upkeep of tile floors. In certain climates, tile can feel extremely cold underfoot.

CONCRETE

Pros: Waterproof and durable, decorative concrete is a new, practical surface that offers a unique look. Generally poured on site into a prebuilt frame, concrete floors can be tinted, stained, etched, and embedded with smooth bits of glass or rock to create a custom application suited to contemporary or spa-styled baths.

Cons: Concrete is a cold, hard surface that can make a space appear harsh and austere if not mixed with other warm design elements. Depending upon the finish chosen, sealing and polishing may be required to maintain the surface. Concrete flooring is pricy and labor intensive. In rare cases where the surface does not set properly, the entire process must be repeated to get satisfactory results.

Above

Large floor tiles in soft, contrasting colors are durable and have an attractive patina that will age well.

TILE STYLE

Tile is a decorative and durable material that has graced beautiful bathrooms for centuries. Bathroom tile, prized for its practicality and versatility of design application, is suitable for a variety of surfaces including floors, countertops, showers, tubs, backsplashes, walls, and even ceilings.

Right clockwise
White marble tile reflects light; a metal finish on a concrete tile looks chic; small glass mosaic tiles are great as a splashback around a stone sink.

Above
A mix of large floor tiles and small mosaic tiles on the wall, combined with the color of the tub, make a serious design statement.

From large squares of tumbled Italian marble that add stunning texture to a stone bathroom, to translucent glass mosaic tiles that make up a sleek, shimmering countertop, tile offers countless applications to suit every style. Though tiles come in a dazzling array of colors and configurations, the majority of material used in residential construction falls into one of the following basic categories:

GLAZED CERAMIC

Made of a clay base with a glaze baked onto the surface, ceramic tile is the most common and widely available type of bathroom tile. It is rated on a scale of one to ten according to hardness. Class one tile, the softest, is best suited for interior wall applications; tile with a rating of class five or higher is considered durable enough to stand up to heavy residential foot traffic. Check its durability before making your selection.

GLAZED PORCELAIN

A more durable version of ceramic tile, glazed porcelain is less prone to chipping and cracking than basic ceramic tile. Glazed porcelain tile is made from a blend of dense clay and minerals fired at extremely high temperatures. Subject to the same hardness rating as ceramic tile, porcelain products are designed to maintain color and appearance even after several years of heavy wear.

STONE TILE

Rich texture and unsurpassed beauty make natural stone tile a time-honored choice among bathroom building materials. While the rich variation in color, texture, and veining is

part of the unique appeal of limestone, marble, slate, and granite tile, homeowners should be aware that these attributes may result in a look that is different from samples viewed in the showroom. Consider hand-selecting tiles for a consistent look throughout. Stone tile is generally available in either a polished finish that creates a reflective surface or a soft, matte finish that absorbs light. Though stone is durable and long-wearing, certain types may require routine sealing.

TERRA-COTTA

Warm and rustic, the charm of hand-crafted terra-cotta (or "saltillo") tile comes from its irregular shape and uneven texture. Common to Mediterranean climates, this type of tile is porous, unglazed, and far less durable than porcelain and ceramic varieties. Accordingly, terra-cotta tile is not the best choice for floors, where heavy foot traffic and increased exposure to water could lead to cracking and staining. However, it is an excellent accent for walls and backsplashes.

Above
The floor and walls of this divine bathroom are tiled with British Racing Green marble tiles, which set off the impressive silver claw foot on the bathtub.

RECYCLED MATERIALS

Tile made from recycled materials is one of the fastest-growing segments within the sustainable building movement. Choices range from eco-friendly glass tile made from reclaimed lightbulbs and windshields to colorful, water- and slip-resistant rubber tile fashioned from radial tires. Just a few years ago, these products were costly and limited in terms of style and supply. Today, however, recycled tile is affordable and widely available in an ever-expanding range of superb materials and fabrications.

GLASS

Architectural glass tile is an increasingly popular option in the bathroom because of the depth, dimension, and visual variation it adds to vanity tops, walls, and tub and shower surrounds. For safety, select industrial-grade, shatterproof glass tile designated for the construction industry. In the past, glass tile was limited to watery shades of blue and green. However, high demand for new products has led to manufacturers' expanding their lines to include a broader spectrum of stunning colors, custom art glass tiles, and interesting new grooved, etched, and iridescent finishes.

Left, Below
The beauty of 1-inch square Italian glass mosaic tiles is shown here. Wall tiles are a mix of green & copper. The floor features a mix of 2-inch square bronzed and black tiles.

Left

Custom-made
mirror-fronted
cabinets and the
white suite stand
out against the
mysterious green
and blue tiled wall.
Low-voltage
halogen
downlighters
located in the
ceiling provide
moody lighting.

DESIGNING WITH TILE

When planning your bathroom, you will realize that no other design element conveys the look and feel of a new bathroom better than decorative tile. Tile has the ability to transform an ordinary wall into a work of art.

Begin the tile selection process by choosing several tile samples that match the mood of your new bathroom. Create a spa-like aesthetic by following one of today's top design trends: large floor-to-ceiling squares of granite, limestone, marble, or slate that line the walls with natural texture.

To give a new bathroom vintage character, classic hexagonal ceramic floor tiles add authentic period detail that connects a newly remodeled space to a decades-old structure. For a more contemporary look, use opaque glass tiles embedded with tiny lights to form a showstopping countertop that softly illuminates a powder room vanity. Or, use the backsplash area to convey a specific design theme, such as a row of embossed seashells in the bathroom of a beach house, or etched-glass tiles that echo a design motif found in other rooms in an Arts & Crafts-style home.

Also consider the size and character of your space. Make a small bathroom appear more spacious by choosing a design using large, light-colored tile and keeping intricate patterns and elaborate designs to a minimum. To scale back a bigger bathroom, install an inlaid floor border 12 inches from the wall to add interest and intimacy. Take that notion one step further to create an elaborate stone mosaic medallion in the middle of the floor that becomes an opulent focal point to visually lower a high ceiling. In a dark bathroom without the benefit of natural light,

Above

Blue and white is a classic color scheme. Here, subway tiles combine with accent dark blue field tiles.

glossy or glass tile forms a reflective surface that instantly brightens the room. Conversely, in a large, sunlit space, tile with a matte finish will neutralize the sun's rays to establish a tranquil mood.

When choosing tile, also think about how much maintenance it will require. Thin grout lines and smooth surfaces are easier to maintain than intricate, molded patterns that require regular cleaning to retain their sparkle.

With prices that range from a few cents to several dollars per piece, designing with tile can be affordable or quite pricy, depending upon the material you select, the cost of labor, and the complexity of the design. As a compromise, keep within a small budget by choosing an inexpensive field tile as the primary material and using more expensive accent pieces to create an eye-catching border. Most tile showrooms employ experts to assist in creating palettes of coordinating bathroom tile designs. Be sure to take along exact room measurements and samples of other materials that you intend to match.

Once tile options have been narrowed down, request samples of each pattern to take home and view in a variety of lighting conditions before making a final decision. This also allows you to see the tile within the scale of your bathroom, away from the distractions (and size) of a tile showroom.

Finally, when you place a tile order, add on a few extra pieces from the same color batch so that you have replacements on hand in the event that a few are accidentally damaged during the application.

TILE TERMS

FIELD TILE

THE PRIMARY TILE USED TO COVER THE LARGEST PORTION OF THE TILED SURFACE, EXCLUDING TRIM AND ACCENTS.

MOSAIC TILE

SMALL TILES, OFTEN SOLD IN SHEETS, USED TO CREATE INTRICATE SURFACE DESIGNS OR LARGE, OVERALL PATTERNS.

ACCENT TILE

A SMALL OR ELABORATE PIECE THAT IS PAIRED WITH FIELD TILE TO FORM A BORDER OR INSERT THAT ACCENTUATES THE OVERALL DESIGN.

BULLNOSE

A CURVED TRIM TILE THAT FORMS A FINISHED, ROUNDED EDGE ON A COUNTERTOP OR WALL.

GROUT

CEMENT USED TO FILL THE JOINT BETWEEN TILES.

COUNTERTOP TRENDS

When you think countertops, think natural materials. Most appealingly, stone's unique composition means that no two applications, hence no two bathrooms, will be the same.

The popularity of stone surfaces has also inspired designers to simulate the look and feel of natural materials in man-made materials. Solid surface, engineered stone, and laminate surfaces offer imitations that mimic the color and style of real materials. Although some man-made surfaces are as expensive as natural materials, the benefits of imitations include better durability and easier maintenance, and a wide range of colors, styles, and custom shapes.

In contemporary baths, concrete is a top trend, offering interesting color variations and versatile textures and patterns that sets it apart from other surface materials. Special pigments mixed with portland cement create stunning colors that range from quiet neutrals to brilliant blues.

Glass is also one of the trends. The latest countertops feature a thick layer of glass suspended above a table or vanity for a reflective surface that literally glows, especially when lit from beneath. Glass is often etched, sandblasted, and patterned in any number of custom motifs.

SELECTION

Start the process by matching the characteristics of each surface with the room's design. Compare features, then narrow the choices by price, lead time, and the level of maintenance required.

With the trend toward luxurious materials, stone surfaces deliver the look that everyone loves.

STONE

Pros: Slabs of solid stone cut to a template of the vanity, with a detailed edge are at the top end. More affordable are stone tiles, set onto a plywood substrata to make the countertop. Choices include granite, marble, limestone, slate, and soapstone. Color and quality vary from piece to piece.

Cons: Periodic sealing is required to protect stone from moisture and prevent stains. Perfumes, nail polish, and cleaning products may damage stone; it requires maintenance.

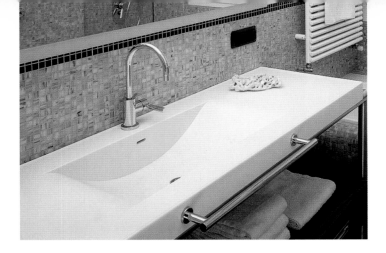

Above

Laminates can be shaped into almost anything. Here, an all-in-one sink and vanity with a smooth finish includes storage.

Left

This is a custom-designed trough sink and countertop made of cast concrete with a smooth country-style finish.

CERAMIC, PORCELAIN TILE

Pros: Affordable and durable, special edge, border, and backsplash tiles customize the countertop. Installation is fast; tile can be set in one day and grouted the next. Single damaged tiles can be replaced.

Cons: Tile grout is susceptible to stains and cracks and requires regular cleaning and sealing to maintain its appearance. Ceramic and porcelain tile is durable but it is not impervious; the surface can chip or crack.

SOLID SURFACE

Pros: Made from natural materials bonded with strong polymers, solid surfaces are smooth, seamless, waterproof, and easy to maintain. Manufactured in several colors and textures, they may be customized with inlays, decorative edges, integrated sinks, and backsplashes.

Cons: Comparable in price to stone, solid surface has a synthetic look when compared to natural materials. Damage that cannot be buffed out may have to be professionally sanded or patched to restore the surface.

GLASS

Pros: Tempered glass is available in translucent styles that enable light to pass through the surface, or opaque countertops that diffuse light for a softer effect. Glass is non-porous, stainproof, and easy to clean.

Cons: Glass shows fingerprints and requires daily cleaning and wiping. It is not repairable; any crack requires replacement of the entire piece.

CONCRETE

Pros: Poured on site, it can be finished to the luster of polished stone, textured, or embellished with stone, glass gems, or leaves. Its finished surface ages well.

Cons: Concrete is a labor-intensive and expensive surface. Cabinets must be reinforced to support the weight, and surfaces require resealing once or twice a year. It can stain and crack as it settles.

ENGINEERED STONE

Pros: Composed of stone aggregates mixed with pigments and acrylic, it is consistent in color and pattern. The product delivered to your home will match that selected in the showroom. Acrylic binders add durability and stain resistance.

Cons: It lacks the character of natural materials. Its hardness and durability are derived from the aggregate used to manufacture the product, so durability will vary by brand. Check with individual manufacturers for care instructions.

PLASTIC LAMINATE

Pros: Laminate is affordable, and improved quality, new color options, textures, trims, and accents make it appealing. Laminate counters are easy to maintain and last well.

Cons: This surface will warp if water gets in beneath the surface. Laminate is prone to surface scratches and is not repairable.

THE VANITY & CABINETRY

Whether you select a handsome metal table topped with a captivating vessel sink, or luxurious wood cabinetry with a lustrous glazed finish, the vanity makes a design statement that establishes the overall tone of the bathroom. See the selection in this chapter for inspiration.

VANITY DESIGN

From its practical beginning as basic bathroom storage, the vanity has risen to prominence. As the master bathroom increases both in size and luxury, the vanity establishes the style.

Left
A custom-style sink with an interesting texture stands alone in a Zen-like room.

Opposite
Wood with a beautiful grain has been made into a countertop for a stone bowl in a country-style powder room.

Left
A traditional white pedestal sink looks crisp against the dark-veined marble on the walls of this elegant Art Deco bathroom.

The days of squeezing two small sinks into a boxy vanity cabinet and calling it a master bathroom are over. Today's large, lavish retreats have expanded to include spacious storage, either concealed within beautiful wood cabinetry or exposed for all to admire, that anchors the design.

Vanities are vailable in every imaginable size, style, and design influence; the keyword is customization. From top-of-the-line hand-crafted cabinet "suites" made to precise specifications, to stock units mass-produced to fit standard spaces, nearly every vanity installed today includes at least one feature that echoes the unique style of the home owner. Differing door styles, specialty hardware, furniture moldings, and curvy new shapes have banished cookie-cutter cabinets that lacked character and definition.

Following is a summary of current bathroom design trends.

BEYOND THE BATH

The emergence of the bedroom retreat that includes space for sleeping, dressing, exercising and relaxing means that storage requirements have evolved over the last decade. Larger spaces call for custom-designed bathroom cabinet suites that provide design continuity between the different function areas. Today, along with the vanity, cabinet components may include elegant built-in dressers and armoires, linen-closets, shoe and accessory drawers, a home safe, a media center, and perhaps a small refrigerator to hold chilled drinks.

SEPARATE SINKS

For some, luxury means more personal space within the room for grooming. That is why many people are opting for separate vanity areas, which increase privacy, efficiency, and practicality in a two-person bathroom, particularly when partners also share the same daily schedule. Install the vanities on opposite walls of the bathroom or, in a larger space, perhaps add a partition with vanity units built on either end.

WARM WOOD

Rich texture and unique grain patterns are two reasons why wood cabinetry continues as the dominant design influence in both new and remodeled bathrooms. Today's trends call for cherry, dark maple, and certain varieties of oak cabinets in traditionally styled baths. For a more modern look, black walnut, sycamore, and exotic veneers from renewable resources in South America and Asia create a more contemporary feel.

CURVE APPEAL

Graceful curves replace straight lines and square edges in another emerging trend: the round vanity. Designs include freestanding units with curved sides and standard vanity boxes with bowed doors. In either case, the gentle profile provides a fresh romantic take on conventional cabinetry.

AGED TO PERFECTION

Paint glazes, dark stains, and hand-rubbed finishes are just a few tricks that cabinet-makers use to prematurely age new vanities and add character that translates to the popular European look. Paint glazes and finishes are a way to achieve an antique look without the fuss of hand-carved details. Overall, expect to see less ornamentation on the current vanity unit, and more emphasis on color and the type and quality of the finish.

Above

An all-in-one sink and countertop made of limestone sits on a cabinet base made of canary wood. The sink's patina becomes more lovely with age.

THE CONSOLE TABLE

Freestanding tables offer an alternative to traditional cabinet boxes. In this case, a piece of furniture, fitted with plumbing and fixtures, replaces the conventional cabinet to create a distinct look in the bathrom. For example, use a brushed-zinc table topped with a glass vessel sink to convey the look of Zen-like tranquility. A downside of this look is that freestanding vanities often mean sacrificing valuable under-sink storage, which makes them a perfect choice for powder rooms or less-used guest bathrooms.

RETRO CHIC

Scandinavian style, fresh from the 1960s, is back. This time around, some furniture manufacturers offer a complete bathroom in a box that includes a selection of sleek, chic vanities in a range of standard styles, along with an assortment of coordinating storage pieces. Many can be purchased in stores or online and delivered to your door. In most cases, the furniture can be assembled and installed in a weekend. Stylish, hip, fun, and affordable, these vanities are perfect for basic bath makeovers and shoestring budgets.

COUNTERTOP CABINETS

Installed at counter level, new vanity tower cabinets improve bathroom efficiency by adding practical storage where it is needed most: at the sink. Open shelving or enclosed shelves provide storage for grooming essentials and small appliances such as hair dryers, razors, and toothbrushes. While the cabinet box is generally matched to the vanity base, the addition of glass-paneled doors adds interest and creates striking style at eye level. Glass also reflects light and makes a room seem bigger.

Above
Chrome supports to this sink and vanity unit add a French flair to this bathroom.

Above left
The contrast of warm wood with the white of a ceramic sink adds an elegance to this country bathroom.

CABINET BASICS

Familiarize yourself with the basics of cabinet style early in the design phase to understand the many options available. Knowing about construction, materials, and quality will steer you toward the best vanity for your budget.

Fluctuating humidity levels in the bathroom indicate that solid wood cabinets may not always be the best choice. Depending upon the size of your bathroom and the proximity of the vanity to the tub and shower, you might also like to consider wood-faced cabinets constructed of plywood, particleboard, and MDF (medium-density fiberboard), all of which tolerate moisture better than solid wood.

While most decisions are driven by budget, other factors are also important. For example, the size and space limitations of remodeling an existing bathroom could limit the choice to a custom-built cabinet that fits the exact shape of the room. Be aware that higher prices may not necessarily mean better quality. Varying degrees of workmanship can be found at all price levels, and from every manufacturer, so do your research before making a final decision.

Though conventional vanity cabinets are available in a broad assortment of shapes, sizes, functions, and finishes, nearly all fall

Right

This impressive vanity unit is made of solid alder wood stained dark mahogany. The Emperador marble has an ogee edge, and is fitted with an undermount sink. The chic Gothic-style faucet is finished in satin nickle.

COMMON CABINET TERMS

FACE-FRAME

A CABINET STYLE THAT FEATURES A ONE- TO
TWO-INCH HARDWOOD FRAME VISIBLE AROUND
THE FRONT FACE OF THE CABINET BOX.

FLUSH-INSET

THIS IS WHEN DOORS AND DRAWERS FIT
WITHIN THE CABINET FRAME TO CREATE A
SEAMLESS SURFACE.

FRAMELESS

(ALSO KNOWN AS FULL-OVERLAY.) DOORS
AND DRAWER FRONTS FIT FLUSH AND
OVERLAY TO THE EDGE OF THE CABINET BOX.

EXPOSED HINGES

VISIBLE HARDWARE PLACED ON THE OUTSIDE
OF THE CABINET DOOR, HINGES OFTEN
COORDINATE WITH HARDWARE AS A
DECORATIVE DETAIL OF THE BATHROOM.

CONCEALED HINGES

ATTACHED TO THE DOORS ON THE INSIDE OF
THE CABINET TO GIVE A CLEAN-LINED LOOK.

TOE KICK

THE RECESS AT THE BASE OF THE CABINET
THAT ENABLES A PERSON TO STAND WITHIN A
COMFORTABLE DISTANCE OF THE UNIT.

BACK PANELS

A SECTION OF FACING THAT COVERS THE
WALL BEHIND THE CABINET AND ADDS EXTRA
STABILITY TO THE VANITY.

The selection of materials for the cabinetry might include maple (white, pickled, and natural), cherry, hickory, walnut, oak, birch, and alder wood; a proprietary manufactured product such as Corian that can be molded and shaped to individual specification to create seamless countertops with integrated sinks; stainless steel that can be made into cutting-edge designs; and MDF with a variety of finishes, including a laminate.

Countertops can be made of any material as long as it is waterproof, or can be made waterproof with a sealant. **Semi-custom vanity cabinets** feature the best of both worlds: design flexibility and superior quality. Semi-custom cabinets are

Above

Modular units like this box design are good for small bathrooms. Dark wood, stainless steel, and a glass sink combine in a sleek design.

Right

This is a traditional style of vanity and sink unit that is still popular today. The drawers and cupboards are more than adequate for storage.

into three distinct categories: custom, stock, and semi-custom cabinets.

Custom cabinets are those built specifically for your bathroom. They are designed to fit the space and are outfitted with features and finishes selected by the home owner. Since they are built to specification, custom vanities have the longest lead time; typically, there is about two months between the time of the order and delivery. As a result, custom-built cabinets are also the most expensive, offering superior craftsmanship and an excellent range of storage options.

At this price point, features to expect might include a hand-applied finish of your choice, plus integrated storage features such as a built-in clothes hamper, tilt-out makeup trays, a slot for the hair dryer that is plugged in through the back of the cabinet, and perhaps a locked jewelry compartment.

factory made and can arrive within weeks. Most manufacturers offer a range of options and modifications that enable their products to conform to just about any bathroom style or layout. These cabinets offer greater design freedom, and the ability to create a unique space with personalized storage options for less than the cost of a custom vanity.

Stock cabinets are mass produced in a few basic sizes and are designed for standard bathrooms. These cabinets are reasonably priced and available in a limited selection of decorative options, door styles, and hardware. Qualities include hardwood frames that are bolted rather than glued, concealed door hinges, and water-resistant finishes.

Construction varies from one manufacturer to the next so it is best to compare the quality of units before buying. For durability and sturdiness, choose cabinets with plywood veneer frames, and look for particleboard shelving that is faced with melamine or laminate.

Whichever type of cabinetry you decide on, consider how much maintenance it will require. Here are just a few questions to ask yourself before you decide: Will the countertop mark too easily and therefore require daily cleaning? Will it chip if you drop a heavy item onto the surface? Remember that the ingredients of some makeup, perfumes, exotic bath oils, and cleaning fluids can damage surfaces that are sensitive to chemicals.

And, a sleek limestone countertop might look fabulous when it is first installed, but unless you treat it with a waterproofing sealant, it will look stained within weeks.

GOING UP

OVER THE LAST SEVERAL YEARS, THE VANITY HAS BEEN REACHING NEW HEIGHTS. BATHROOM CABINETS THAT ONCE STOOD A STANDARD 30 INCHES TALL ARE NOW BEING RAISED A FEW INCHES HIGHER TO REDUCE BENDING AND TO ACCOMMODATE TALLER PEOPLE. THE NEWEST BATH DESIGNS FEATURE VANITIES THAT RANGE FROM 33 INCHES TO 36 INCHES AND BEYOND. INCREASED PERSONALIZATION OF THE BATHROOM MEANS THAT SOME DESIGNERS NOW CUSTOMIZE THE VANITY TO CATER TO THE HEIGHT OF THE HOMEOWNER. IN A TWO-SINK BATHROOM, THIS COULD MEAN THAT ONE SINK MIGHT MEASURE 31 INCHES FROM THE FLOOR, WITH THE OTHER INSTALLED AT 37 INCHES FROM THE FLOOR. THIS LATEST TREND OFFERS FURTHER EVIDENCE THAT THE PRIMARY FOCUS OF TODAY'S BATHROOM IS ON THE CURRENT HOMEOWNER, RATHER THAN THE FUTURE BUYER. IN ADDITION TO COMFORT AND CONVENIENCE, TALLER VANITIES ADD EVEN MORE STORAGE, A WELCOME BONUS IN ANY BATHROOM.

STORAGE

Finding adequate storage in the bath has always been a bit tricky. The question of where to put towels, cosmetics, the hair dryer and other essential bathroom accessories is easily answered when you plan storage to fit the space.

Left
These storage spaces appear to float in space between the countertop and cupboards.

Above
A space beside the cabinet is perfect for storing rolled towels in colors that harmonize with the natural stone and the warm, dark wood tone.

Until recently, bathroom storage amounted to a few narrow vanity drawers and under-sink cabinets obscured by plumbing. However, carefully planned storage systems integrated into bathroom design plans from the start ensure that every square inch of space is efficiently utilized.

Just as the size of the average bathroom has nearly doubled in the last two decades, so have storage requirements. In addition to stowing bath essentials like towels and toiletries, today's multi-tasking spaces require personalized storage for items such as jewelry, makeup, and clothing as well as more modern amenities like exercise gear, sound systems, and the latest bathroom desirable, flat-panel television screens.

The best way to approach storage is to begin thinking about it even before design plans are drawn up. Your current bathroom will provide clues as to what you may need in your new space. Take a look at systems that function well in your current bathroom, and

STORAGE 101:
BUILD A BETTER BATHROOM

THE KEY TO CREATING A SERENE SPACE IS SELECTING STORAGE FEATURES THAT HELP STREAMLINE TASKS AND ACTIVITIES. INCORPORATE THESE SMART STORAGE SOLUTIONS IN YOUR PLAN:

► CREATE SLIDE-OUT STORAGE BY FILLING THE EMPTY SPACE BETWEEN VANITY CABINETS WITH A SIX-INCH PULLOUT UNIT OUTFITTED WITH CUSTOM RACKS FOR SCARVES AND NECKTIES.

► LATEST BUILT-IN CLOTHES HAMPERS FEATURE A LARGE, REMOVABLE BASKET INSERT THAT LIFTS IN AND OUT FOR EASY TRANSPORT TO THE LAUNDRY ROOM.

► INSIDE THE DRAWERS, ADJUSTABLE DIVIDER UNITS RANGE FROM SMALL COMPARTMENTS FOR MAKEUP AND MEDICINES TO LARGER ONES FOR CLOTHING AND LINENS.

► SPECIAL TILT-OUT TRAYS INSTALLED BELOW THE SINK TIP OPEN TO REVEAL SPACE TO STORE MAKEUP, AN EXTRA PAIR OF EYEGLASSES, OR DENTAL SUPPLIES.

► RACKS MOUNTED TO THE INSIDE OF VANITY DOORS KEEP UNDER-SINK STORAGE CLEAR BY ORGANIZING CLEANING SUPPLIES, TISSUES, AND SOAPS IN A CONVENIENT PLACE.

► NEW BATHROOM DESIGNS INCLUDE MORE VANITY DRAWERS, AND FEWER CABINETS WITH DOORS. THE REASON? DRAWERS OFFER FLEXIBILITY AND MAKE BETTER USE OF LIMITED STORAGE SPACE.

► TAMBOUR (GARAGE-STYLE) STORAGE UNITS ALSO WORK WELL IN THE BATH. INSTALL ONE AT THE BASE OF A COUNTERTOP CABINET TO STORE HAIR DRYERS, RECHARGEABLE RAZORS, AND ELECTRIC TOOTHBRUSHES.

► CONTEMPORARY MEDICINE CABINETS COMBINE STYLE WITH PRACTICAL STORAGE FACILITIES, AND CAN FEATURE DEEPER SHELVES AND BUILT-IN LIGHTING TO MAKE SEARCHING AT NIGHT EASIER.

duplicate them in the new design. Then come up with a wish list of features that you want to incorporate in the new space. The idea is to create storage tailored to day-to-day basics as well as the additional activities that take place in the retreat.

For example, linen storage is a basic requirement in every bathroom. To address that need, one designer came up with a two-sided storage closet with access from both ends. One side opens to the tub and shower area, the other side opens to the exercise room. The same bathroom features a small reading bench with a slide-out drawer for resting paperbacks and magazines, as well as a slim CD rack that is recessed between wall studs.

Regardless of the size or configuration of your bathroom, every room—from standard to superior—has unused space that can be outfitted with storage to improve function. For example, valuable under-sink storage that is sacrificed with a pedestal sink or console table might be made up by adding open

shelves to empty wall space behind the door. A tiled niche built into a shower surround carves a shampoo shelf out of previously unused space. A glass-fronted tower cabinet placed on top of a traditional vanity adds visible and accessible storage to an empty stretch of countertop.

For the budget-conscious, lining a wall with open cubbies is an affordable way to add storage without the expense of fitted cabinetry. In addition to cutting costs, cubbies and other styles of open storage save space by eliminating the clearance necessary for cabinet doors to swing out into the bathroom.

Think of storage as the backbone of your new bathroom, and the key to a pleasing, well-organized space. The most thorough way to plan storage is to divide the room into function zones and evaluate each of them with the idea of placing items close to where you will use them.

The four basic bath zones include the shower and tub area, the sink, the closet or

Above left
Small units on wheels are handy to move around the bathroom.

Above right
Cabinetry that hangs off the wall is a chic, modern design trend.

Opposite
Storage in this light-filled bathroom is hidden behind the lacquered white floor-to-ceiling cupboard doors.

dressing room, and the toilet. Larger retreats will have extra zones to reflect different amenities. However, the planning process remains the same: make a list of the items that will be used or stored within each zone, then choose storage solutions that fit each task.

Some examples: If two people use the area at once, building a pair of small walk-in closets, rather than one large space, works better for the morning rush. Or, if you enjoy glancing at the day's headlines during your daily workout, consider a media cabinet outfitted with a motorized lift. In these custom units, the television rises out of the cabinet at the touch of a button and lowers back down out of sight when not in use.

For practicality and future resale of the property, every room should have flexible storage capacity to suit most households.

GET ORGANIZED

MOVING INTO A NEW MASTER BATHROOM IS THE PERFECT TIME TO MAKE A FRESH START IN A NEW SPACE. SEIZE THE OPPORTUNITY TO TAKE STOCK OF YOUR BELONGINGS, LET GO OF WHAT YOU NO LONGER NEED, AND PLAN EFFICIENT STORAGE FOR THE ITEMS THAT YOU ACTUALLY USE ON A REGULAR BASIS. TAKE A CUE FROM PROFESSIONAL ORGANIZERS WHO FOLLOW THESE STEPS TO SORT, SEPARATE, AND SET UP ORGANIZATIONAL SYSTEMS.

► SORT THROUGH CLOSETS, DRAWERS, DRESSERS, AND VANITIES TO ELIMINATE THOSE ITEMS THAT HAVE NOT BEEN USED OR WORN WITHIN THE PAST 12 MONTHS.

► SEPARATE UNWANTED ITEMS INTO TWO CATEGORIES: THOSE TO DONATE TO CHARITY AND THOSE TO DISCARD.

► SET UP SIMPLE STORAGE FOR THE REMAINING ITEMS. MOST FREQUENTLY USED BELONGINGS SHOULD BE ACCESSIBLE AND PLACED AT EYE LEVEL; LESS FREQUENTLY USED ITEMS CAN BE PLACED ON HIGHER SHELVES.

TO MAINTAIN A SENSE OF ORDER IN YOUR NEW BATHROOM, REPEAT THE PROCESS ONCE A YEAR. YOU MIGHT BE AMAZED BY HOW MUCH MORE YOU HAVE ACQUIRED.

HARDWARE

Bathroom hardware is one design detail people overlook. Yet the hardware is the final touch to a successful decorating scheme.

In design terms, whatever the style of your bathroom (Period or Contemporary), all the hardware must be the same for consistency of style. There are literally thousands of styles and combinations to select from and you will find that when you select a faucet style, there is usually a range of hardware to match it.

The term "hardware" covers all of these items: tissue holders, towel bars (single and double), towel rings, robe hooks, soap dishes, toothbrush holders, electrical switch plates (from single to quadruple), door handles, shower door pulls, and cabinetry knobs and pulls.

If you are selecting grab bars, check they meet ADA (American Design Association) requirements and that the screw (or other type) fitting is well made so it will not come out of the wall after a few months.

Finishes range from the classic polished chrome, stainless steel, solid brass, and pewter to satin nickel, oil-rubbed bronze, and antique copper. If you like the weathered iron in rust or black, make sure these fittings are powder coated over solid brass so they will not leave marks on your towels.

For a vintage look, try a classic set of designs available from restoration stores, such as a polished chrome-and-glass soap-dish holder, and a vintage train-luggage–style rack, featuring generously proportioned ball finials of drop-forged brass and exposed hardware that pays faithful homage to the 1930s originals. It also stores towels.

For a contemporary look search for styles by well-known product designers such as Philippe Starck, Norman Foster, Michael Graves, Phoenix Design, and Massimo Iosa Ghini.

In Starck's latest range, a simple hook carries the glass lamp shades as well as the paper holder, the glass shelf, the toothbrush holder, and the circular towel ring. The latter is big enough even for large bathroom towels. Accessories, too, are reduced as much as

Clockwise

Elegant shaping in a chrome hand-towel ring; 1930s chrome towel rack; a sophisticated Bordeaux-style towel ring; and a clever use of space is shown here with a Craftsman-style towel ring, door handle, and matching pulls.

they can be. Toilet brush sets are designed to be both wall-mounted and floor-standing; the twin-towel holder and the bath-towel bars can also be used as support grips.

From a designer's point of view, cabinetry handles can make or break a vanity unit. If the handle looks out of place with the rest of the fittings, it will immediately draw the eye to it. These are the small details that can spoil a decorating scheme.

When you look at items such as these in a store it can be confusing, so perhaps buy one of the design you like, take it home to the bathroom, and place it on the cabinet that might be its final resting place so you can check if the proportion is correct and, above all, if its finish is suitable for the other fittings.

LIGHTING

A well-designed lighting plan makes it possible to comfortably use one space for a range of routine activities. In this chapter, learn how to improve the quality of natural light in your bathroom and how multiple layers of artificial light change the character of a bathroom retreat.

NATURAL LIGHT

Natural light creates a captivating ambience that lifts the spirit and brightens the mood of any room. In the bathroom, the amount of light impacts virtually every design; surface materials appear to shift color throughout the day.

Though the location of the bathroom within the home determines how much natural light the room gets, borrowed light and strategic placement of windows and skylights are tricks that architects and designers use to manipulate light and enhance interior spaces.

Ideally, the bathroom will have at least one exterior wall with large windows that provide plenty of light and a connection to the outdoors, without sacrificing the privacy of the room. If the home's location precludes privacy, the next best scenario is to install window treatments or diffused glass to obscure the view into the room. Or you can locate windows above eye level, close to the ceiling. When space permits, you could consider an enclosed "gazing" garden just outside the bath. A three-sided wall, or trellis built onto the side of the home, provides instant privacy and brings light, as well as a glimpse of the outdoors, into the bath.

Any bathroom can be brightened with the help of one or more of the following architectural features:

Right

Placing a large mirror near a window can more than double the quality of light, which will bounce around the room and, depending upon the time of day, create amazing light plays to watch as bright light settles into shadows on walls and floors.

SKYLIGHTS

The easiest way to bring natural light into the interior when windows are not an easy option is to install one or more skylights to highlight a feature of the room. In hot climates, adding an automatic blind to a skylight will keep the room cooler by blocking out the midday sun. Although many skylight designs are manufactured to be kept permanently sealed, there are versions that can slide open to improve ventilation.

skylight. Installed on the roof, these work by capturing sunlight and directing it through a tube that runs through the attic and rafters to the ceiling of the interior space. Solar tubes offer the benefit of natural light without the heat often generated by skylights and are considered a good solution for dressing rooms and walk-in closets where UV rays can fade clothing and furnishings.

SLIDING PANELS

Inspired by Japanese Shoji screens, sliding panels are an ingenious way to create a light, airy feel while increasing the usable space of a master retreat. When open, the panels slide into a storage compartment located inside the wall. When drawn, etched or sandblasted glass panels establish privacy, yet still allow natural light to filter through.

INTERIOR WINDOWS

When structural or budget constraints prevent the replacement of a wall, installing interior windows between the bathroom and the bedroom is a less disruptive means of improving light for a fraction of the cost. Place windows high enough on the wall to ensure privacy and position them toward an exterior exposure.

GLASS DOORS

A low-cost solution to adding more light is to replace solid wood interior doors with clear glass-paneled French doors, which will pull light into darker spaces.

GLASS BRICKS

Replacing a section of interior wall with glass bricks adds a touch of luxury that brings light into the center of the home. Consider creating a custom application with versatile new shapes and tinted colors.

SOLAR TUBE

Solar tubes bring light into spaces that do not have the direct roof access necessary for a

ATMOSPHERIC LIGHTING

Light creates atmosphere, provides orientation, and directs our gaze to what really counts. Whether you are remodeling or starting afresh, a lighting plan is the key to enhancing special features in a bathroom.

Since wiring for fixtures takes place in the early stages of building and remodeling, it is never too soon to begin thinking about lighting. Having a plan in place before work begins will prevent unnecessary delays once the building begins. The bathroom is unlike any other room in the home. Reflective surfaces, a lack of natural light, the ceiling height, and multiple activities are just a few of the challenges that may require extra consideration when you are planning the lighting. Lighting design also plays a supporting role in conveying the overall style of your space.

A lighting plan begins with an evaluation of each zone. First, when it comes to the number of light fixtures in your plan, it is best to err on the side of too many, rather than too few. Dimmer switches and adjustable controls make it easy to tone light down if necessary.

Since much of the conceptual planning takes place from a set of blueprints, a professional lighting designer versed in bath design and the latest in lighting technology is an invaluable resource. He or she can guide you through the process of selecting the fixtures and styles that address the specific requirements of your space.

Basic advice to do-it-yourself people: To avoid shadows, use bathroom lighting fixtures that use diffusers to cover the incandescent bulbs. These types of bathroom fixtures radiate flattering light and color. Position sconces on both sides of the mirror at least 28 inches apart, and 60 inches above the floor. To surround your face with light, install a fixture 24 inches wide over the mirror.

Above
Small LED lights have been set into floor tiles to create a unique design and light the way through the area to the tub in this contemporary European design.

STEPPING OUT OF THE TUB OR SHOWER TO TOWEL DRY BENEATH THE WARM, GENTLE RAYS OF A THERAPEUTIC HEAT LAMP IS A SMALL, HOTEL-STYLE LUXURY THAT IS MAKING ITS WAY INTO THE MAINSTREAM OF RESIDENTIAL BATH DESIGN. HEAT LAMPS ARE EASY TO INSTALL AS A STANDARD CEILING FIXTURE AND DELIVER EFFICIENT, LOCALIZED HEAT DESIGNED TO TAKE THE CHILL OUT OF THE AIR AND CREATE A SOOTHING SENSATION IN THE BATHROOM. SPECIAL INFRARED BULBS WARM UP QUICKLY TO RADIATE AMBIENT HEAT IN A MATTER OF SECONDS. FOR SAFETY, ADD A WALL-MOUNTED TIMER WITH AUTOMATIC SHUT-OFF AND, IN SMALLER SPACES, SELECT FIXTURES THAT COMBINE A HEAT LAMP AND VENTILATION FAN.

Above

In this bathroom, two beautiful round lamp shades are well placed on either side of the mirror to enable sufficient lighting for the face.

A well-lit master bathroom should incorporate the three basic types of lighting: ambient, task, and accent. In smaller spaces, blending different intensities of light brings out the best of the room by adding depth and dimension that would otherwise be lost in the darker shadows.

The next step in the lighting plan is to ensure that each activity area has adequate lighting to perform specific tasks. Finally, the plan ought to include accent lighting.

In period bathrooms, select the fittings to match the style of the rest of the home. Victorian, Art Deco, Classic, Retro—each of these styles is well represented in lighting showrooms. Chrome, bronze, brass, and other metals are combined with clear or frosted glass shades and can be bought as a single unit, in pairs, or in up to four or five fittings set along a strip that can be attached to either the vanity unit or the ceiling.

Wall sconces are also manufactured in a myriad of traditional and contemporary designs to match the style of any bathroom.

Downlighters for use within a shower are also manufactured with finishes including chrome, gold, nickel, and stainless steel. Check that the unit you buy displays the

Above

Period light fixtures are available to match the surroundings, such as this polished chrome and opaque glass design in an Art Deco hotel bathroom.

safety rating given to fixtures which come into contact with water or other objects.

There are innovative mirror products on the market, too, which use a dual lighting system. When you approach a mirror, an integrated motion detector switches off the diffuse interior light and activates the actual mirror lighting. The contents of the cabinet vanish from view and the previously transparent mirror surface now shows the mirror image of the person standing in front of the cabinet.

Floor tiles set with LED (light-emitting diode) lights transform the humble tile into a light source. The LED is an electronic component and, as a light source, offers high luminosity, extremely low energy consumption, and low thermal emission.

Familiarize yourself with the characteristics of each category of lighting, and then bring your room to life with fixtures that fit specific functions and radiate the style of the bathroom space.

AMBIENT LIGHTING

Ambient (or overall) lighting is installed in the ceiling to softly illuminate the entire room. Proper placement of these fixtures is crucial to avoid glare and shadows in the bathroom. Ambient lighting usually generates enough light to comfortably move about the room; however, it lacks the intensity required for task areas. Use one ambient fixture for every 50 square feet of space.

TASK LIGHTING

Vanity lighting must be bright enough for men to shave or women to apply makeup, yet be soft enough to flatter skin tones. Most lighting designers recommend light strips either on the top or along both sides of the mirror to eliminate any shadows and fully illuminate both sides of the face. Another design option is to place wall sconces at eye level on either side of the mirror, or use a flexi-arm fitting by the mirror so you can direct the light where you need it most.

At the vanity, use color-corrected fluorescent or incandescent bulbs that emit a softer light that balances skin tones. Use task lighting to enhance tub, shower, and toilet zones of the room. Over the tub, a recessed ceiling fixture set on a dimmer switch can shine brightly for reading, or be turned low for a more subdued setting.

ACCENT LIGHTING

This type of decorative lighting highlights a specific architectural feature, or creates a focal point in a room. Accent lighting also adds drama and is a subtle means of delineating different zones of the bath. Use fittings inside glass-paneled countertop cabinets to illuminate a piece of sculpture, or beneath a glass vessel sink to add a soft glow to the room.

CHROMATHERAPY

The theory of color therapy is based on our natural reaction to the color of light. Therapists have been using color as a healing tool for decades. Only recently have technological advances meant the systems can be installed in a home.

Chromatherapy is based on light-changing systems. Color-changing lighting works by mixing (usually) three hues of color in varying amounts. It works because the white light source is made up of different wavelengths, each having a degree of color. Therefore, if white light can be split into, say, red, green, and blue (RGB), then it follows that RGB can be turned back into white light. Turn down the red a little and white light becomes yellow, turn down the blue and yellow becomes green, turn up the red and blue and turn down the green and you get a magenta tone, etc. In other words, depending on the mix and strength of each of the red, green, and blue light you can create any shade of light.

RGB lights are manufactured as fluorescent strip lights (for instance, you would have one red, one blue, one green strip); as fiber optics, where a light source mixes the RGB colors; as tungsten lightbulbs, and as LED (light-emitting diode) format. LED lighting is suitable for bathrooms because it requires a low voltage (about 24 volts on average) and the bulbs can last for 100,000 hours or more.

Chromatherapy lighting sets the mood like no other type of lighting. It can be installed in ceilings and walls and in floor tiles and other types of flooring. Some bathtubs and shower stalls are made with chromatherapy systems pre-installed for an instant light show *(see Showers, page 79).*

You could place the fittings around the top ledge of a bath surround and watch the ceiling change color. You could also set fixtures in the floor in front of the bath panel, in a towel warmer, and around or under a sink for additional special effects. Setting a light show inside the shower in a vertical row will light up the glass in a changing parade of color; you could also place fittings in the top or leading edges of steps in a bathroom.

Whatever you select, ensure you have a fully qualified installer to fit it and, if you are in doubt, take advice from a specialist.

Above

A shower stall such as this one from Europe is fitted with a pre-installed lighting system that can change the color experience of a daily shower at your fingertip command.

FIXTURES & FITTINGS

In this chapter you will discover, once again, how the small details can make or break a decorating scheme. Choose the right showerhead, the best faucet for the comfort of your fingers, and the right bathtub for the way you live, and the dream will be completed.

SINKS

Sinks are not just receptacles for water—they have become countertop vessels of fashionable status.

China, porcelain, glass, stone, stainless steel, gold plate, and acrylic materials are used to manufacture sinks for all purposes. There is even a sink made from a stretched polymer that makes a drumming sound as the water hits on the taught-skinned surface.

The first thing to do is to decide what sort of sink you want, and how you are going to mount it. Is it for one or two people? Do you want it to hold just a small amount of water or copious amounts? Does it need to hold water or is it just for a running mix to rinse hands or clean teeth? Are you going to use its edges for storing toothbrushes, soap, and a facecloth?

Then, decide if you are a round or square person. Do you prefer a discreet undermount sink, or do you prefer a sink to be on display? Having decided its position, consider the space you have available and how the sink is to be fitted. Will it be on a pedestal, wall mounted, or set onto a useful storage base? A sink set onto its pedestal creates a traditional look. Pedestals are used not only to help support the sink but also to hide pipes and waste fittings and can be fashion statements themselves.

Increasingly, sinks are wall mounted, with waste fittings that have been specially designed to be seen under sinks set directly onto a wall. Check with your local plumbing supplier for more information on styles. Sinks that are set into units or directly into cabinetry are a practical solution for small spaces. This is also a good way to hide unattractive pipe work.

Left
A colored undermount sink presents a smooth finish to a smaller vanity.

Right
In this contemporary and shallow sink, water flows down the tray into a hidden drain.

Current design trends feature both wide rectangular and the smaller, rounded sink shapes. The bathroom décor is the key to deciding the sink's shape. If the room features hard edges and straight lines, then a rectangular sink is the best choice. If the room has curved edges and softer lines, then a rounded shape will suit the décor. A traditional bathroom in a Victorian house will be perfect with a classic pedestal sink, classic polished chrome faucets, and towel bars of the same design period.

Given the variety of sinks manufactured, your sink is bound to be available. The last important piece of advice concerns cleaning it. When you've found the one you want, check how easy it is to clean, and if the surface is prone to scratching. Despite advances in cleaning materials, some surfaces will wear more than others. Because a sink is used so often, this durability issue ought to help you make the right choice.

Left
A new concept features a glass integrated sink with a single mixer.

Right
Undermount sinks are still popular, as seen here in this calm bathroom located at the beach.

THE TUB

Bathtubs are grouped into two categories: soaking tubs and whirlpool, or air jet, tubs. Do you look forward to beginning your day with a citrus-scented soak? If so, consider a soaking tub that enables you to add bubbles, oils, and salts that would damage the jets of a whirlpool tub. However, if you like pulsating jets of water to massage weary muscles, a whirlpool, or air jet tub, is the one for you.

Once you have chosen the type, check plans for bathroom measurements. If you are remodeling, the tub must be small enough to carry through halls, stairways, and doors that lead to the room. Also, when you install to a larger tub, you have to upgrade to a bigger hot water tank. (Bigger tubs can drain a standard water tank before the tub is filled.) If this is not possible, install a second water heater just for the bathroom.

Among popular styles are tubs for two built on site and faced with tile, stone, wood, or concrete. Other examples include luxurious overflow tubs placed in the middle of a bathroom with plumbing leads that run up through the floor. Expensive tub designs include soaking tubs sculpted of translucent acrylic, and cushioned seating.

Basic tub styles include sturdy drop-in tubs in a choice of materials and finishes for a reasonable price. For a bit more, opt for an extra-deep freestanding tub with a durable finish, and sculpted contours for comfort.

Whirlpool and air jet tubs circulate water by way of a motorized pump. The size of the tub determines the horsepower needed to move water through the system; larger tubs require more powerful motors. A big-capacity whirlpool will run in the range of 50 GPM

The restorative powers of a relaxing bath are legendary, which is why homeowners list a deep and luxurious bathtub as one of the most desired features of a new bathroom.

(gallons per minute) with a 3-horsepower motor. Look for quiet operation.

Here is a summary of materials from which tubs are manufactered.

ENAMELED CAST IRON

Cast iron tubs can weigh as much as 500 pounds (without water) and may require floor joists to be reinforced to provide support. Made by spraying a durable coat of porcelain enamel over a metal base, these tubs are solid.

Above

Freestanding tubs are frequently found in the limelight of a luxury bath. The classic French-style tub matches the wall tiles behind.

ACRYLIC

Tubs made of acrylic can be molded into any number of shapes, allowing design flexibility. The tubs resist chipping, provide excellent insulation, and retain heat for long periods.

ENAMELED STEEL

By far the most common postwar bathtub construction is a molded steel tub finished with a tough enamel coating. These hardy and efficient lightweight tubs are still available in a wide variety of colors, although they are now often replaced by more modern materials.

CULTURED STONE

Made of stone aggregates mixed with acrylic, cultured stone tubs have the look of natural materials but cost less. Molded in one-piece units, these are sold in standard and custom units in faux stone textures. They wear well.

FIBERGLASS

Also referred to as gelcoat tubs, these are the cheapest, least-durable models. A coat of acrylic is sprayed over a reinforced fiberglass base; the finish is prone to scratching and dulling. They do not last more than a decade.

Above

A double-ended tub designed by architect Norman Foster. His design is made of acrylic material cast between two polished glass sheet plates and has nonporous surface that resists bacteria.

BATHTUB STYLES

Alcove Tub Designed to fit into a niche surrounded by three walls, alcove tubs are made in 5- and 6-foot lengths.

Clawfoot A freestanding tub supported by sturdy legs and installed with exposed plumbing. Traditionally made of cast iron.

Corner Tub A large tub placed on an elevated platform in a corner of the bathroom. Also referred to as a garden tub.

Drop-in A bathtub set into a custom, built-in frame and deck structure faced with tile, wood, or stone.

Frame Tub A modern update of the clawfoot, frame tubs are freestanding fixtures suspended in a wood or metal frame.

Japanese Tub A small, deep tub designed for sitting upright, rather than lying down. Traditionally made of wood, but new models are also available in acrylic.

Overflow Tub This option includes a tub-within-a-tub; a continuous cascade of water flows over the edge of the inner enclosure into a surrounding sink.

Pedestal Tub A design that is freestanding. Instead of legs, it rests on an oval pedestal base that sits directly on the floor.

Tub Shower Combo Good for small spaces, this is a one-piece unit that includes a bathtub, shower, and wall panels.

Above

Sheer luxury seeps from this infinity tub made from acrylic material and toughened glass.

Left

A sculpted acrylic tub features unique removable and adjustable supports for the head and upper back area.

SHOWER POWER

Much more than a cleansing cascade of water, the shower is now a technological force that sprays your body from every imaginable angle.

"Rejuvenate" and "revitalize" are key water therapy words. The latest shower enclosures also enable you to answer the telephone, watch television, listen to the radio, and enjoy a color light show *(see Chromatherapy, page 71),* while your feet are automatically massaged. Here's what's available in one enclosed unit:

• Steam function • Chromatherapy
• Handheld shower • Body jets
• Accupressure massage wall-panel jets
• Foot massage unit • Ceiling spray
• Computer control panel • Stereo speakers
• Steam time and temperature control
• Telephone • FM radio • Light functions
• Interior light • Extractor fan • Built-in seat

Some of the latest shower stalls feature flat, wide-screen LCD television and a heated mirror inside the shower.

Also, a powerful hydrotherapy massage can be yours at the turn of a faucet. Body sprays can be incorporated into the columns of the stall, directing water back into the cabinet. In wet rooms, where everything can get wet without worry, the number of jets you can set to pulsate your body is limited only by the size of the hot water supply. The ultimate in bathroom retreats features a steam environment where couples can relax together. A steam shower helps you sleep and work better by relaxing your body, increasing blood circulation and metabolism. The warm, moist air helps relieve tension and muscle pain. All steam baths are made with remote function and are constructed of toughened safety glass.

Showerheads are available in a wide range of designs. Waterfall styles, where water cascades over your head and your shoulders, have therapeutic benefits. At the top of the price range, there are heads with a central light outlet illuminating the water as it exits the shower head. Set a sequence to change the color as the water flows.

New showers have sidelined doors and feature a simple section of glass, fitted to prevent major splashing into the room. Where a door is necessary, the trend is for no-frame doors—panels of glass fitted directly to the tiling or stone walls and floors, and door hinges fitted directly to the glass surface.

Above

Adjustable spray settings in the newest shower cabinets include wide, needle jet, rain, champagne, and massage. You can imagine which pressures this shower might feature.

TOILETS

More than ninety percent of all toilets are made of white pottery and come in a range of styles, shapes, and sizes. Although there are other types, the majority are either round or egg shaped. The old-fashioned variety with tanks set high above the bowl have long been replaced and can only be obtained from specialists. Basically there are three variations, which are widely available:

A conventional floor-standing two-part tank and bowl combination.This is the most common type, where the bowl and tank are separate items but coupled together to create a single unit. With the focus on ecological friendliness, newer models work efficiently with much less water than earlier models, consuming 1.6 gallons per flush compared with some of the recent models with a half-flush option.

One-piece toilets are made from a single-molded pottery shape which incorporates the tank, bowl, trap, and skirt into one seamless unit. These vary in height and depth but many models have a low profile and incorporate modern styling.

Less common, but becoming more popular, are **wall-hung** and **concealed-tank** toilets. These models incorporate a separate tank which is built into the bathoom cabinetry and are operated by either a flush lever or by a push-button air valve. They are also very quiet in operation because the water filling occurs behind a wall. Wall-hung models need a special steel framework which must be very securely attached to the wall and floor.

Above

A traditional toilet suite in white is perfect for the veined white marble used on the floor.

DESIGN TIPS

Select a toilet suite that suits your bathroom's design and fits comfortably into the space available. There are toilets available for tight areas such as smaller bathrooms and powder rooms. Some are simply reduced in length; others can work from the corner instead of a flat wall so they protrude at a 45° angle into the room.

TOILET SEATS

SOME ADVANCED SEATS FEATURE A PNEUMATIC VALVE WITHIN THE HINGE AND THIS LETS THE SEAT AND OR LID GENTLY DOWN BY ITSELF. HEATED TOILET SEATS HAVE NOT PROVEN AS POPULAR AS THE MANUFACTURERS THOUGHT THEY WOULD BE, PERHAPS BECAUSE MOST HOMES ARE HEATED DURING THE WINTER.

TOILET SEATS CAN ALSO MAKE A DESIGN STATEMENT. SOME ARE MADE FROM CLEAR, SOLID ACRYLIC AND REVEAL SEASHELLS AND OTHER ITEMS SEALED SAFELY WITHIN THE ACRYLIC.

THE ULTIMATE DESIGN COMES FROM JAPAN. WHILE YOU ARE SEATED, A MOTORIZED DOUCHE SPRAYS WARM WATER AS A BIDET WOULD, THEN GENTLY BLOWS WARM AIR ONTO THE BODY TO DRY IT.

FAUCETS

A faucet can achieve a synthesis between form and function, which is important when any type of disability is taken into account.

Sink fillers/mixers/faucets are perhaps the most important statement in a bathroom. Their design says more about the bathroom than anything else because everyone touches, uses, and feels the response of a faucet. The way the handles turn, how the water flows, how well it mixes hot and cold, and how easily the speed and temperature are controlled are important to a user.

Faucets are manufactured in many styles and finishes. Polished and matte chrome, solid gold, stainless steel, pewter, silver plated, brass, satin nickel, silky aluminium, bronze-effect . . . the range can be confusing if you are a first-time buyer.

Mixers rule, with single or twin levers. These are made as monobloc (all-in-one unit) or in two-hole or three-hole pieces. The ultimate unit is a four-part bath filler consisting of hot and cold faucets, a spout, and a pull-out shower attachment.

Spouts are now also available as shallow glass dishes, open-faced designs that pull up and out and retract after use, and spouts that swivel.

For a small bathroom, select a wall-mounted fitting to preserve space. Economy of design, striking shapes, and interesting finishes also help a small bathroom. Currently the most popular trend is for something slim, sleek, and with the finer details and the finish making the design statement.

You can speak to a faucet and it will activate; hold your hand a few inches away from it and water instantly flows. Select from levers, dials, slide controls, knobs, glass stems, jewel-encrusted handles to activate; there is a range of faucets that are activated when your knee pushes against the sink vanity door. The latest faucets feature spouts with light emitters that let you see water coming out without turning on the light. Some designs sport a ring of light emitters around the spout; in others, the water gushes from an open slide that has light behind, and/or underneath, for effect. As the temperature changes, the light subtly changes from blue (cold) to red (hot).

Ask a plumber about the types of valves used in the faucet you like. There are two types of valves: compression and ceramic. A compression valve features a washer, and is the type that's been used for decades. Ceramic valves feature ceramic discs that are virtually indestructible and are commonly used in modern fittings.

Above
A 19th-century design with a weathered brass finish fills a sink.

Left
More French classical romance in this luxurious Cygne design.

Below
Water as sculpture in the bathroom; a fountain for relaxation.

PART TWO

CASE STUDIES

MIRACLE SPACE

Venice Beach is the location for this ensuite bathroom.
Adjacent the master bedroom in a house alongside
one of the canals, its curvaceous form seduces the
bather into its invigorating environment.

Left

The circular shape
introduced by the
wrap-around wall is
repeated in the
double sinks. The
faucet is an Arne
Jacobsen design.

Above

Vibrancy zings off the
shower wall which is
covered with glass
mosaic tiles. the
shower fitting is a
modern classic design
in a polished chrome.

Opposite

A continuation of
the frosted glass
wall wraps itself
around the tub to
create a division
between the
passageway and
the ensuite.

Opposite

The perspective
from the master
bedroom shows
the relationship
between the
exterior walls and
the opaque glass
wall wrapped
around the tub.

Love at first sight? Sensuality and luminosity, two romantic notions, are combined in this refreshingly honest ensuite bathroom designed by architect Glen Irani for his outstanding canalside home.

On closer inspection it is the incredible lightness of being there that captivates; the density of the accent colors makes their presence come into focus against the white backdrop.

The architect, one of the modern Californian architects making their mark on the architectural landscape, explained how the space plan works.

"It's an efficient plan, with little wasted space. The tub anchors the whole, even though it's sandwiched in a wrap of glass and you actually enter it from the end. This looked like a big mistake on paper, but it works in reality very well."

The tub keys off the vanity cabinet, which ended up being only 20 inches high, so the double sinks were elevated on a custom-bent frosted acrylic plinth. This makes a stylish design statement, as the photographs reveal. To save depth in the small space the faucets, the Vola design by Arne Jacobsen, are mounted on the wall.

All of the private facilities such as the toilet, bidet, and shower are concealed behind a wall of frosted glass, creating a luminescent backdrop for the vanity area.

Above

The tub, nestling
into its glass
surround, gets full
sunlight in the day.
Once in the tub,
the bather is snug
in the enclosure.
The polished
concrete floor
reflects the play
of sunlight, too.

► Designed for light and energy in the morning

► Circular design theme

► Mosaic tile in shower area

► Polished concrete floor

► Plaster and paint finish on walls

Above

Polished concrete and frosted glass plus a splash of strong color and chrome fittings combine to present a simple but very effective design.

Morning light from the east showers the space with warm sunshine, therefore fulfilling his wish for a bathroom to invigorate him every morning with daylight, color, water, and beauty, plus refresh his half-sleeping body and mind. Bright orange mosaic tiles in the shower add to the awakening.

The master bathroom had to fit into a very narrow space that was compressed by the access corridor and the light-court outside, so the thin frosted-glass partitions gave back almost 18 inches of width for him to work with when designing.

The light and sparseness lend to the sense of ample volume despite the diminutive 60-square-foot floor area of the vanity space. The functional compartments serve as luminescent backdrops to the main space, being partitioned in frosted glass and backlit by sunlight in the day and by artificial light at night. His desire was for the bathroom to "become a lantern for the master bedroom. I wanted it to glow like an immense candle, hence the frosted glass everywhere, backlit with soft incandescent light." De Rosa pendant globes provide this softness more than adequately.

This is clearly the bathroom of a man who considers the details in depth.

"Design is all about life. Exercising a rigid intellectual process is like being imprisoned and shackled to something much bigger and more static than architecture requires." Therefore, he tries to focus on each pertinent factor in each unique project and try to freely imagine solutions that are both functional and romantic.

The house in general is an expression of Glen Irani's interest in manufacturing. Manufactured items fit, working beautifully and with precision. The man-made stuff he likes is fun, colorful, intelligent, minimal/essential, and ergonomic. As an architect, he dislikes products that are dysfunctional and misornamented.

"I think my home expresses my dream that one day tooling will be accessible and affordable so that I can manufacture my buildings rather than have them built."

Above

A luminescent backdrop to the double sinks is created by the countertop unit and the thin frosted-glass partition wall.

Right

The vanity unit is made of MDO (medium density overlay plywood) with an acrylic coating, upon which sits a molded support for the sinks. Walls, other than in the shower, have a painted finish.

"Serenity" is the most appropriate word to describe the ambience in this thoughtful bathroom in the home of a California-based furniture designer and his wife. Each fitting and fixture has been chosen to reinforce the concept envisaged by the word "retreat."

Right
This is the view into the bathroom from the exterior courtyard where the owners's favorite fish, the Japanese carp, leisurely swim in a landscaped pond.

SERENDIPITY

Above
Natural stone has been used as a strong surface for both walls and floors, creating a brilliant textural effect and making a firm design statement.

Right
East African wenge wood, with all of the ethereal qualities it brings to a room, is the perfect foil to the natural stone elsewhere in the bathroom.

Coming into the house where this bathroom resides is like walking into an oasis of calm amidst the chaos, and the bathroom is at the center of this calm.

The owners, furniture designer Nick Berman and his wife Debbie, were very focused on exactly what the space should look like, and how it ought to be constructed.

The Bermans wanted to create a sanctuary that would not only inspire them but still provide them with all the functions they required, yet without sacrificing the feeling of intimacy they both wanted.

The bathroom is divided in two by the tub and the shower, and the division is further emphasized by dropping the floor level of the shower and covering it with small mosaic glass tiles. This gave more architectural prominence to the separation between the unique vanities, too.

The stone wall and floor surfaces elsewhere are made up of slabs of Northern

Left

An Asian influence dominates the dressing room where dark wood and light-colored stone meet like East and West. The exterior views are never far away.

Above

The beauty of dark wood grain is simply stunning in this solid cabinet. The unique drawer pulls are made of hand-forged steel with a pewter finish.

DESIGN SUMMARY

▶ Main wall and floor surfaces are of Native Idaho quartzite

▶ All cabinetry custom made by Nick Berman

▶ Natural materials emphasize the retreat mood

▶ Natural light dominates

▶ Earth tones in color scheme

▶ Sunken tub for soaking in peace

Below

A deep soaking tub
is sunk into the ground.

Idaho quartzite in Sunset Gold tones. The stone, along with the natural-looking grouting, produces a cool and calming influence. To further emphasize the tranquil feeling, the Bermans placed a water element on the same center axis as the tub and shower so when they are in either, and the glass pocket door is fully retracted into its pocket, they feel as if they are bathing outside. They can also see their favorite koi lazing around in the pond.

The tub surround is made of dry stacked stone and harks back to a tradition of countryside stone walls. The surround is capped with a smooth stone ledge, into which the faucet is set.

In a furniture designer's home, every item of furniture is important and it is especially so in this retreat. It was Nick Berman's intention for each of the specially crafted new cabinets to look as if it had just been found and put in this serene place. His clever plan worked, for each of the magnificent units appears to have centuries of karma imbedded in its soul.

The major stair-stepped storage unit is Nick Berman's interpretation of a Tonsu chest, and is built as a single unit using flat-cut East African wenge. As you can see in the photographs, it has a superb, rather coarse texture that looks good when used decoratively and wisely. It has a clear lacquer protective finish.

"I have never been to Asia but I feel a connection to its culture," he said.

The connection is real enough. This storage unit is an impressive piece of woodworking, the sort of fine-quality piece you would expect to find in a place as serendipitous as this.

Right
Water flows from a faucet fashioned from marble. It takes 120 gallons to fill this tub.

SET IN CONCRETE

Building materials come into, and can quickly go out of, fashion. However, concrete is eternal, especially when it is used to such grandstanding effect in this 400-square-foot space by an architect for a theatrical client and his partner.

Left
A polished chrome faucet designed by Philippe Starck is perfect for the carved limestone countertop.

Opposite
An exposed mechanized system of pulleys raises maple blinds from pockets in the floor beneath all five of the windows to provide privacy.

Right

Three simple stalls
line the sidewall,
providing shower,
toilet, and sauna
facilities. The
storage unit is
made from canary
wood.

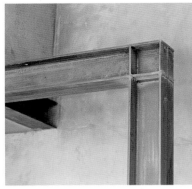

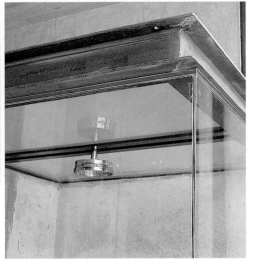

Opposite

Bathe in dappled
sunlight while
taking in the day's
news beamed via
the flat-screen
television.

For the architect Leonardo Chalupowicz, creating a master bathroom as an addition to the West Hollywood home of Milton Katselas was the result of a creative partnership between the architect and the client, a theatre director and artist. They had met through a mutual friend and discussed design ideas. Later, Leonardo Chalupowicz was hired to design his kitchen. It had always been the director's dream to create a sanctuary, with lots of space and filled with light.

When the house adjacent to Milton Katselas's home became available, he bought it and razed the existing house to the ground. In its place has arisen a master bathroom worthy of any superlatives used to describe it.

In this case, the client was the design partner for the project. "A lot came from Milton," said Leonardo Chalupowicz. "He has created his castle."

The master bathroom was part of a more extensive renovation project, during which Milton Katselas remained on site. "His watchful eye was helpful in moving it along. It was a painful but useful experience."

The duo went to great lengths to site the addition in a place where is could not be overlooked by the apartment building to the north. Clever landscaping also helped to achieve this.

Left

Chic polished chrome fittings, including a handheld shower, fit neatly in the control center by the sunken tub.

The use of materials was experimental in that the steel beams were uncoated and left to rust; the plaster on the walls was an exterior plaster and its natural patina has intensified with the humidity; and the polished look of the concrete floors has aged well.

For Leonardo Chalupowicz concrete is a noble, expressive material which, even though it is heavy, "has a lightness about it and is, in the right hands, full of possibilities. I was interested in coming up with something where you could see the hand that made it."

Both men had a vision of a roomy and sunny, light-filled retreat with state-of-the-art spa facilities within an industrial environment. This atmosphere begins when the suspended steel door rolls across the entry from the master bedroom. To the right is a bay of five windows which wrap around a sunken, colored concrete tub, cast in situ, positioned for the morning sunlight. Along the side wall are three stalls: shower, sauna, and a toilet. Opposite is a limestone-topped vanity with cabinetry made of canary wood. Close by is an ofuro, a Japanese soaking tub constructed of eucalyptus wood.

The floor is cast in a high-density insulated concrete with a polished finish, and the walls have a hand-troweled plaster finish. The wood ceiling is constructed with planks of blond Douglas fir. A striking feature is the rusting steel beams which, when you look closely, still bear the marks of builder's tools.

Being attentive to detail, the duo built a styrofoam life-size mock-up of the tub to ensure the idea was sound, and that it was located in the right place. More attention to detail can be found in the choice of a steel shutter in the sixth bay area that can be cranked open by hand for ventilation. Leonardo Chalupowicz deliberately incorporated the rattling sounds made by the equipment when in use because they added to the soul of the room. The sounds also fit with Milton Katselas's fondness for honesty in all artistic mediums.

DESIGN SUMMARY

➤ Polished concrete floor

➤ Smooth hand-plastered wall finish

➤ Sunken tub sited for light and sun

➤ Rusting steel beams on display

➤ Retreat-leisure ambience

Left

Set in prime position is Katselas's classic pony-skin Le Corbusier chair, just in case he wants to catch a television program.

Opposite

The Japanese ohuro (soaking tub) is constructed of eucalyptus wood.

THE GUEST'S SPACE

DESIGN SUMMARY

▶ Cylindrical shape open at the top

▶ Glass blocks allow light in

▶ Stainless steel fittings

▶ Rough concrete finish

▶ Smooth floor features water drain

Architect Leonardo Chalupowicz used even more creativity when it came to designing the guest bathing facilities.

The result is a combination of powder room and shower designed as a cylindrical enclosure and measuring 8 feet high and 5 feet in diameter. Again, both client and architect pushed the boundaries of construction, casting the concrete for the cylinder in a mold generally used for water mains. Its rough surface (left as is, straight from the mold) adds an edgy feeling to the concept of an early morning shower.

Right

Concrete and glass bricks create a personal temple within which honored house guests can shower, and day guests can visit.

Left

The beauty of the planks of the Douglas fir ceiling can be seen through the light-giving area at the top of the cylindrical enclosure.

Light, more than enough to shower by, enters the well through the open top and also through a tall, narrow window of glass blocks. A stainless steel sink, a narrowing cylindrical shape as it reaches the floor, adds more utilitarian mood here. A flexible, small mirror is placed at face height. Water drains away through a central point in the floor. Its soaring shape evokes an almost religious architectural quality. Is this personal sanctuary perhaps a mini temple, the ultimate homage to the ritual of beauty? Sparse in its amenities, utilitarian indeed, but ultimately beautiful?

Above

Looking into the annex where the shower, separate toilet room and sitting area are located. A black-and-white framed photograph demands attention.

A conversation between the owners of this new home, architect John G. Reed and interior designer Marisa Solomon, over two sinks and a tub in a bathroom showroom, set the tone for this master bathroom.

This was to be a merger of two minds. The architect creates contemporary spaces, and the designer prefers traditional lines. John Reed loved the sinks and Marisa Solomon adored the Empire tub, and a deal was done.

When designing their master bathroom, it was important the space be large enough for them both to feel like they had their own personal space. Marisa Solomon also wanted the floating Empire tub to be the focal point.

The bathroom is designed as a retreat from the rest of the home, with three separate spaces, each with a different function, that flow together and create the illusion of a larger space. A dressing area separates the

Right

White terry-cloth covers were designed for the chairs in the annex to create a cozy, inviting seating area to sit and relax after a bath, shower, or massage.

This master bathroom, elegance personified, is owned by a couple who combined their architectural and design talents to create a comfortable space for bathing.

MARBLE CHIC

Right

Finishes in the
bathroom are a mix
of wood, marble,
white porcelain,
and polished
nickel. Note the
different marble
detailing at floor
level.

bedroom from a closet and the bathroom, creating a formal entry into each space. The main area is designed with two pedestal sinks and a mirror polished nickel tray table set against a wall of Carrara marble. Opposite the two sinks is a floating Empire tub set against a wall of glass overlooking the garden and waterfall.

Dark hardwood flooring (5-inch hand-distressed walnut planks with a custom stain) creates continuity between bedroom dressing area, closet, and main bathroom area, and also provides a strong contrast between the marble walls and white tub. The floor material changes to a basket-weave marble floor outside the shower (not shown). The feel of this shower space is also much cooler and totally different from the main bathroom.

John Reed explained: "The design challenge was to combine contemporary plumbing fixtures and cabinetry, clean lines, materials that worked in both modern and traditional spaces, architectural woodwork and moldings, and carefully selected antique pieces reflecting both our design ideas."

The antique chandelier and antique perfume bottles also give the contemporary space a traditional touch.

As a result, the bathroom is a space they both love and are very comfortable with.

"There's nothing we would have done differently," Marisa Solomon said.

Opposite

The reflection of
the French doors
in the leaning
full-length mirror
visually increases
the size of the
room and brings
the outside in.

DESIGN SUMMARY

▶ Honed Carrara white marble on walls and the floor in the shower area

▶ Polished nickel finish fittings

▶ Custom-stained walnut flooring

▶ Ash wood recessed cabinetry with dark espresso finish

▶ Chandelier and wall sconce lighting

Above

The large and deep acrylic Empire-style tub is the centerpiece in this area of the bathroom. One of the pleasures is laying in the tub with the doors open, listening to the waterfall sited outside.

Above

Dark American walnut cabinetry creates a wonderful contrast to the soft tone of Turkish limestone.

Left

The toilet set is attached to the wall to allow the floor to flow freely. Note the small light-fitting set into the floor.

Opposite

The flow of walnut from the floor up the wall is a major design feature. Hidden in the side (not seen here) is a slide-out storage cupboard.

SURFACE WINNER

Here is an example of how good design can create a truly unique space. Textural and light plays make this bathroom a winner in every sense. Each surface has been designed, then finished, to blend harmoniously with all others.

Left + right
A ceiling curve
delineates where
old and new start
and finish.
Limestone and
American walnut
create a smooth,
luxurious look.
A unique water
spout can fill the
bath from above.

This discreetly elegant contemporary
bathroom was designed to seamlessly blend
into what is, historically, a part14th- and
part16th-century wood-framed house in the
county of Suffolk, England.

Interior designer Andrew Bannister of
Design Republic was faced with an exciting
challenge. His clients wanted something
completely different from the typical Victorian
suites that are often installed into houses of
this period. Because his clients appreciated
design of the finest quality, Andrew was able
to let his imagination turn one part of this
ancient house (the area that partially dates
back to the 14th century) into a tranquil
environment designated for relaxation and
pure pleasure.

As is common in houses of this age,
no two walls in the house were level, square,
or straight. Plus, the ancient structure was
unable to take the considerable weight of the

Right

Downlighters were set into the swath of plaster ceiling for an ambient effect. You can also see the ceiling-mounted bath-filler placed discreetly between the two lights.

Above + right

Small light fixtures are set into the steps leading to the deep tub. They cast a soft, warm glow over the Turkish limestone.

bath when filled, so Andrew and the builders constructed a large wooden cradle coach that was bolted to the outer frame of the building. The bathroom was then designed to have modern elements set within some exposed existing features of the house; the older walls were plastered and painted, and newer walls were covered in limestone imported from Turkey.

The end result shows how the old and new blend together in a swath across the ceiling; a new surface on the ceiling matches the new surface on the walls; and old ceiling surface matches old wall.

The inspiration for the design came from the Japanese approach to design. The theory is that natural materials are blended together to form a harmonious and balanced room where the eye can be drawn to a simple candle, flower, or feature without being overwhelmed by too much detail.

It worked here for Andrew Bannister, starting with his approach to the tub. An overflowing design (the water is pumped in a loop) creates an infinity swimming pool effect in a domestic environment. The water is reheated and you can, at the touch of a

Above + right
The vanity unit is American walnut; the sink is of limestone. Sophisticated design is apparent in the faucet which lets the water flow over a glass edge. A single lever operates the flow.

button, enjoy an underwater color lighting display, and rising tiny bubbles that produce a champagne effect. This is an extra-deep tub that holds 123 gallons and is filled thermostatically via wall valves and from a ceiling spout. A small handheld shower is stored out of sight behind the rim of the tub when not in use.

The sink is manufactured in hand-cut Turkish limestone, and features a superb, award-winning German glass and chrome sink mixer. Water flows over the rim of the glass dish into the sink.

All of the furniture is handmade in American black walnut, including a secret storage area above and to one side of the toilet suite and its concealed tank area. The roll holder was sourced from Italy to add an individual focal point to an otherwise utilitarian accessory.

One of the clever design features is apparent when you walk into the bathroom. As you walk in the door, a black walnut floor leads you to the toilet and then rises up and behind it to the ceiling, creating a stunning contrast against the limestone that covers the floor, and the ancient painted color themes of the walls and the ceiling. The toilet is wall hung so that the flooring can continue underneath it unhindered.

Other design details include a mirror that floats away from the old part of the wall to add a modern contrast against the original lathe-and-plaster Georgian finish.

A tall, heated chrome towel warmer provides heat in addition to that of the underfloor electric heating system. Body, feet, and soul need never be cold in this bathroom.

The radio-controlled lighting is designed to provide light in several separate zones. Ceiling-inserted spots create pools of

light in dedicated areas such as the sink, toilet, and over the bathtub. LED floor lighters illuminate outward from the face of the step between the limestone floor levels, and LED uplighters are situated around the bathtub and at either side of the sink for background ambient lighting.

A combination of these, with the option of the color-changing tub lighting, gives the bather various levels of light, color, and chromotherapy. There are seven buttons for preprogrammed levels and mixes of light on the remote control. That toy is better than a rubber ducky any day.

Above

The extra-deep tub is designed for relaxation and can hold up to 123 gallons; it is filled thermostatically via wall valves and from a spout in the ceiling.

Opposite

A whirlpool tub with an integral waterfall spout features pulsating jets, armrests, and a body spray. The electric window blind above the tub rises and lowers at the touch of a button.

Right

Underfloor heating was planned at an early stage, as was the light fixture under the vanity drawers and doors.

Sweeping views of San Francisco Bay and a seductive setting on a sun-drenched hill made it easy to overlook this Marin County California home's only flaw: a stale layout left over from the 1970s.

The original master bathroom floor plan featured a small toilet and shower wedged into a cramped space next to the master bedroom, while the sink was situated several steps away in a hall corridor. Still, the home's other attributes made the makeover a worthwhile challenge. Wisely, the homeowners decided not to rush into the remodel. Instead, they took their time to consider every detail of their planned retreat.

"Since the layout was the biggest challenge of the project, living in the home before the remodel was the most efficient way to get a clear idea of the functional use of the space," said the pragmatic husband. "Time was less of a factor; the greater issue was getting it right."

Living in the original home for a few years helped to clarify their primary goals. First, the homeowners desired an airy, light-filled master bathroom with two sinks,

SOOTHING SPACE

Luxurious spa-style amenities, superb planning, and divine details spell tranquility in a retreat designed for relaxation.

Above + right

The double shower features an
impressive array of controls and water
jets designed to relax the body.

a separate toilet compartment, a deep
whirlpool tub, and a large walk-in shower.
They also wanted to enlarge the bedroom to
include a sitting area and his-and-hers walk-in
closets with plenty of storage.

Creating the separate task zones
meant a reconfiguration of the entire second
story. Extra space was gained by repurposing
a small office behind the original bathroom
and closing off a section of hallway. Raising
the height of the room to meet the roof line
created a dramatic sloped ceiling, adding
volume and visually enlarging the new room.

Attention was then turned to implementing
features that needed adding during the
building phase. Here, meticulous planning
paid off in the form of a hot water
recirculation pump, a heated floor with a
programmable thermostat, and an extra layer
of sound-absorbing insulation.

Careful consideration of a vast array of
materials samples produced a handpicked
palette of wood and stone that gives the
finished space its warm, contemporary edge.
The starting point for the mood: French
limestone wall tile that extends to the ceiling

to enfold the room in a creamy layer of variegated texture. The smoky, slate-colored ceramic floor tile offers easy care. The vanity's long, polished granite countertop creates a contrast against the matte-finished materials found elsewhere, while just beneath, the cherry cabinetry is a fine example of sophisticated simplicity.

Steps away, the double shower has a built-in bench, two sets of controls, and individual thermostats. In addition to its luxe look and impressive list of amenities, it is the attention to detail that impresses.

Pocket doors preserve space and contribute to the room's sleek style, small toekick lights installed beneath the vanity guide the way into the darkened room at night, and self-closing storage drawers effortlessly retract.

With every comfort considered, the completed master suite is a stunning sanctuary and oasis of calm that the homeowners relish.

Above

Throughout the bathroom, resort-quality fixtures offer spa-style pampering. The wall tile is Mocha Cream honed limestone.

Below

An alcove by the toilet is the ideal place for the telephone, or anything else you might need to hand.

DESIGN SUMMARY

➤ Mocha Cream honed limestone wall tile throughout

➤ Whirlpool bath

➤ Underfloor heating

➤ Electric blinds as window shades

➤ Skylight for added sunlight

DESIGNED FOR A FAMILY & GUESTS

The creation of a new kitchen extension provided the ideal opportunity for a master suite where a dramatic oval skylight gives the bathers a stunning view of blue skies and starry, starry nights.

Left

The oval skylight floods the bathroom with light by day and gives a stunning, starry view at night.

Right

The bathroom has twin built-under sinks divided by glass shelving that provides storage space for an eclectic mix of toiletries and decorative bits and pieces.

DESIGNED FOR A FAMILY **117**

Opposite
page

A mirrored partition
conceals the toilet,
but still allows a
view of the Golden
Gate Bridge
through the antique
leaded window
rescued from the
old staircase.

The family thought that all they wanted was a kitchen extension, but when the architects D. J. Pak and Nestor Matthews of Matthews Studio pointed out that the space could also be used to create a first floor master suite, the idea was too good to resist.

The new rooms above the kitchen extension are shoehorned into a narrow space, but appear light and spacious because of the high, sloping roofline, clever use of mirrors, and the addition of a dynamic oval skylight that more than compensates for the lack of windows in the space.

"When our longtime clients asked us to help them with the extension to their home for a new kitchen, we realized that it made sense to move the master suite upstairs, too," said Nestor Matthews.

"While the addition could only be seven feet wide, we were able to take advantage of the dramatic roof lines to create a bedroom and add the oval skylight in the master bathroom.

"Everything else is rectilinear so the oval-shaped skylight becomes a focal point."

Because the new bathroom is long and narrow, the architects used a galley-style layout with sinks and storage along one long wall, and a shower stall on the other. Bottocino marble in a soft, creamy shade used on the floor and countertops, and in the large walk-in shower stall, sets the subtle color theme. Design highlights come from carefully selected and well-placed decorative pieces in dark wood, nickel, glass, and china.

A fresh orchid adds a splash of vibrant color and is cleverly placed on a dark Oriental tray, providing a dramatic contrast to a striking stone sculpture, by Edwin Neuhaus from the Moderne Gallery in Philadelphia, which draws the eye when you enter the room and infers a spiritual ambience.

The vanity is made of bleached quarter-sawn oak. There is a ceiling light at the vanity, and the lights at the vanity itself are a custom design manufactured in frosted glass. The vanity faucet is a traditional and sturdy design.

Cabinetry cupboards and drawers feature square-shaped recessed handles, which provide an unbroken line, an essential design detail in a long, narrow bathroom.

Above

Ceramic sinks are undermounted into the marble top to give sleek, unbroken lines and are used with polished nickel three-hole faucet sets.

Right
Shower fittings,
robe hooks, and
handle pulls have a
polished nickel
finish.

Remember that bathroom furniture must be resistant to damage from steam and moisture.

The roomy mosaic-tiled shower stall has a wide opening door for easy access and is fitted with a powerful retro-style hand shower. A strong bench-style stool made from Sonoma cypress is positioned just out of the reach of the shower spray so that it can be somewhere to place dry towels close to hand, and also provide a comfortable place to sit while towel drying.

There's also a useful built-in niche for shampoo and toiletries, and the outside of the stall has been drilled to take robe hooks. Building a small partition meant that the toilet could be separate from the main bathroom. It is located right beside a window at the end of the room, but privacy is no problem.

"We were able to salvage an antique leaded glass window to use in the toilet area from the old staircase in the house. The leading slightly obscures the glass, providing

just the right amount of privacy, yet still allows views out to the Golden Gate Bridge," explained Nestor Matthews.

The toilet is one of a range of elegant designs by Philippe Starck, who says he was inspired by the shape of an old-fashioned bucket when he designed this range.

The owners may not have planned to add this bathroom but now that it's in place, they more than appreciate the brilliant flash of inspiration from their architects that extended the brief of the original commission.

Tranquil and soothing, this is a bathroom that's just right for a relaxing retreat from the frantic world outside.

Right
Wall niches are a useful addition to the shower stall.

Above
A contrast between the large floor tile and the small mosaic wall tile adds visual interest, as does the Asian-style stool.

DESIGN SUMMARY

► Natural materials used for walls, surfaces, and floors

► Natural light floods in

► Lots of well-planned storage space

► Mirrors reflect light and the view

Left
The high-style
toilet combines a
slimline tank with a
streamlined bowl.

Opposite
Walls in dry areas
are covered in wood
panels painted in
soft sage while the
area behind the
toilet and around
the tub is covered
in jade green tiles.

GUEST HAVEN

The architects also created a new guest
bathroom for the family. Here, said Nestor
Matthews, squares were the inspiration for
the design.

"We wanted a more interesting
surface than tile on some of the walls so we
decided to do the non-wet areas in painted
wood panels. The rest of the walls are
covered in small square tile with a slightly
larger tile on the floor so we were able to
have some fun with scale."

The subtle sage green tone used for
the painted wall panels is repeated in the
built-in vanity unit which is topped with

man-made Surell solid surfacing, which
continues down the side of the vanity and
along the bath side, making a monolithic,
easy-to-clean surface. Surell looks like real
stone but is lighter, warm to touch and
impervious to heat, abrasion, and impact. It
can be cut, shaped, and routed, and even
used to make inset bowls.

The bathtub doubles as a shower stall,
thanks to a well-fitting shower surround with
a wide opening door for easy access. A
traditional wire storage basket provides
storage space for shower gel, shampoo, and
toiletries, which is an important practical
point that many bathroom designers overlook.

The floor plan for this bathroom meant
that the toilet could not have been hidden
away, so Nestor Matthews decided to make
the most of it by choosing a stylish model
from the Philippe Starck range.

"It is a beautifully sculptural design,"
he said, "and we also chose the faucets
designed by Starck to go with the pure
white sanitaryware."

Stylishly simple, this bathroom is a
welcoming oasis where guests can relax,
refresh, and unwind, and where comfort
combines happily with the straight lines and
pared-down style of modern minimalism.

Below

Custom-made, built-in furniture is fitted with unobtrusive chic recessed pulls by Hafele.

Left

This single-lever faucet was designed to complement the toilet design.

DESIGN SUMMARY

▶ Soft shades of green and cream create soothing atmosphere

▶ Practical easy-to-clean surfaces

▶ Bathtub doubles as a shower stall, saving space

▶ Wood panels add a warm feeling

Nestled on the hilltops above Los Angeles, this home has a view to sigh for, across the valley out to sea. Clever use of space on the upper level, which is devoted to sleeping and bathing, lets you to stand in the shower and enjoy the view.

Left
Morning glory is a view out across the monumental Getty Museum to the ocean beyond.

Right
The view of the small sitting area with a built-in sofa and a television. The colorful paintings are by Eastern European painters, bought by the owners on a recent trip there.

COMFORT ZONE

Opposite

The stone circle mounted on an iron stand is a piece of ancient money from the South Seas region. The U-shaped bench it sits upon is one from the Armani Casa range.

Left

Rift-cut white oak cabinetry is the star of the bathroom. The stack of drawers is made out of one piece to get the grain running all the way up.

This house in the hills was originally built in the 1930s for a B-movie actress, and the current owners are only the second people to live in it. It was the worst house in the best location and they bought it because of the potential, and the view. Its style was "vaguely Paul Williams with some deco touches added," according to interior designer Tim Geutzlaff, who worked with his clients to refurbish the home.

The top floor, of three, consists of a fabulously luxurious bathroom, a dressing room, and a master bedroom. The space to create this new area was created from three existing bedrooms and a bathroom.

The clients both have high-pressure occupations in the visual world that involve lots of travel. They wanted to come home to a crisp and clean environment but one that was still comfortably tactile and enveloping. To help expiate their request, the owners moved into the lower floor guest quarters while work went on above.

All the windows and doors were replaced with double-paned glass with UV protection so no window coverings are needed. All baseboards, window and door casings, crown moldings, and extraneous details were removed. Windows and door spaces were taken full height, from floor to ceiling, to make the floor as open as possible. The home was re-piped and an instant hot water unit installed because the new fixtures required good water pressure.

The original carpet flooring was removed and replaced with 5-inch wide, quarter-sawn, white oak planks finished in a custom warm gray stain that is about three shades darker than the cabinets. The bathroom and adjacent dressing room floor is tiled in 1-inch square glass tiles, which are also used in the steam shower for the ceiling, walls, and floor.

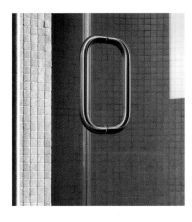

The window wall in the bathroom is finished in Lagos Azul limestone, as is the counter. The surface is honed and sealed to resist staining. Fossil shells appear randomly in the limestone. The window in the shower was originally made of glass bricks, and hid anyone in the shower from view. That wall was widened and the bricks replaced by toughened glass, and the stall became a steam shower with a mirror that doesn't mist over. Music is also piped into the shower

Above

All of the handles and pulls have a brushed stainless steel finish and are seen throughout the house.

stall, as it is around the entire floor, through speakers set into the ceiling.

A range of pale gray-lilac colors that had been used in a remodel of another home Timothy Geutzlaff had done for his clients was expanded to darker and lighter shades and used throughout the house. The "taupe-with-a-dash-of-mauve" walls are darkest in the television area, a shade lighter in the hall

Above

Lagos Azul limestone was used for the counter. The surface is honed and sealed to resist staining. Fossil shells appear randomly in the limestone.

Right

The two sinks are placed far apart in the limestone countertop. Here you can see through to the dressing area. The faucet is a classic design in polished chrome.

area, another shade lighter in the bedroom, and lighter in the dressing room. When you look down the hall, the color recedes, giving a sense of distance. Ceilings throughout are painted a pale gray.

The design dogma here is based on the theory that you see what you need to see and everything else is hidden, out of sight, behind closed doors. All of the cabinetry is made of rift-cut white oak because the grain in this wood is so good.

"A set of drawers is cut from one piece so the grain runs all the way up," explained Timothy Geutzlaff. All the cabinetry is stained medium gray, with a hint of lilac.

One of the owners is in the fashion business and that meant drawing up storage closets to house his entire collection of suits, shirts, ties, and shoes, socks, underwear, and menswear accessories. The drawers in the dressing room feature small, medium, and large partitions in Baltic birch or a combination of maple and birch that are the perfect space for specific items. Two of the cupboards are hampers, one for drycleaning, one for laundry.

The home is now a restful background accented by personal objects and art collected on travels, all fitting within the space, united by color and form.

Oh, and you might have noticed. There is no bathtub. The idea does not appeal to the owners. They are now planning the construction of a swimming pool and spa for total H_2O immersion. Watch this space.

DESIGN SUMMARY

➤ Wall sconces are frosted slumped glass to diffuse light

➤ Dimmers can set different moods

➤ Soothing color range throughout

➤ Honed limestone countertop

➤ Brushed stainless-steel hardware

➤ See-through shower stall

POLISHED ACT

Left
Faucets in a matte finish that complements the Comblanchien Clair limestone top.

Below
Collections dot surfaces around the suite, adding a warm, lived-in look.

An ingenious open-plan design transformed the upper floor on this bungalow into a multipurpose area for bathing, exercising, or simply relaxing. Best of all, it is not just for the parents. The children have their own space in this family suite.

Left
A Japanese Tanzu chest provides storage for towels and toiletries. Its dark wood is picked up in the framing of the family pictures.

Turning more into less has given the owners of this bathroom a light, bright, wide open space where they and their children can bathe, relax, sleep, or simply chill out in one of the cozy seating areas that dot this amazing bathroom and bedroom combination.

Before design team Sheldon Trimble and Nestor Matthews of Matthews Studio started work on a complete remodel of the family home, the upper floor was a collection of smaller rooms. Turning several spaces into one large, interconnected area was an idea that the owners, both graphic designers and brand consultants, loved. Spaces flow seamlessly one into the other, thanks to the summary banishment of dividing walls.

By removing the full wall behind the bed, they were able to bring more light into the bedroom and open up the sitting/exercise space to other activities in the suite.

The living space behind the bed leads to the sink area of the bathroom. A supersize headboard made from stained mahogany screens the bedroom area without cutting it off from the space beyond. The space behind the bed then leads to a walk-in shower and

DESIGN SUMMARY

▶ Freestanding furniture adds a warm touch to the design

▶ Removing walls floods area with light

▶ Limestone floor and countertops

▶ Painted walls

▶ Natural colors complement dark wood

▶ Open-plan design but privacy retained

vanity area, and a separate toilet. Beyond that is a dressing room that overlooks the green and pleasant landscaped garden.

The vanity, a floating custom design, has a ceramic undermount basin in a limestone countertop and it appears to float off the wall. Matte platinum faucets are in harmony with the smooth softness of the limestone countertop. Subtle pull-out drawers are located to the front of the vanity.

Flooring throughout this cleansing area is constructed of durable Comblanchein Clair limestone tiles with a protective finish.

Above

A luxurious duvet cover and colorful embroidered pillow soften the severe dark wood background.

Left

The comfortable
cream-colored
sitting area behind
the bed leads into
the working area of
the bathroom.

The baskets beneath the vanity are antique
pieces from Indonesia and the Philippines;
they provide useful storage in this space.

Freestanding furniture, including an
upholstered seating area and a 1950s
Japanese Tanzu chest placed between the
two vanities (they are opposite each other in
this area), plays a major role in creating the
feel. The architect believes furniture in
bathrooms is good because it makes them
feel less antiseptic and also provides a
counterpoint to all the built-in furnishings
usually associated with a bathroom space.

Right

An elegant light
fixture flanks the
mirror above the
vanity. Positioning
lights at either side
of a mirror gives
clear illumination.

Above

The cute frog tile
adds a quirky
touch to the
practical wall area.
The glazed garden
stool picks up the
colors seen in the
floor tiles.

Above right

The Craftsman
floor tiles were
used to build the
large shower tray
in this walk-in
shower stall. The
hand shower is
adjustable.

FOR CHILDREN ONLY

It's a tough ask designing a bathroom strictly for children. Too adult just won't appeal; too gimmicky means the space won't grow with the kids. Here, the design team managed the perfect compromise for the children, designing a room that is fun and young but has elements that adults will also appreciate.

They wanted to create a modern interpretation of a bungalow bath experience. The floor tiles, in traditional colorways, play off of the clean lines of the vanity.

A spacious shower stall with robe and towel hooks placed on the wall handy to the unit makes showering easy, and the hand shower is on a riser rail so the head can be moved up or down to suit different heights. The sink is built into a custom-polished concrete top, which has been dyed blue. This design decision was taken so that it would relate to both modern and traditional elements in the area.

The oversized doorknobs on the vanity furniture below are a playful reminder that this bathroom is a young person's space.

A frog tile is also a reminder that this is a room for kids. The team ordered one frog tile, and had the clients choose the spot where it was to be installed while the tile setters were standing by. It is attention to details like this that finish a unique design.

Left

Dyed maple was used to make a hardwearing vanity. The base unit is topped by a polished concrete slab inset with a sink.

Below

The letters are the initials of each child's name. The S-design step stool matches the yellow in the glazed tile.

DESIGN SUMMARY

> Craftsman WTC series floor tiles

> Floating vanity design in dyed maple

> Concrete custom-colored countertop

> Tile flooring throughout means splashes do not cause problems

> Cream tile wall in shower brightens up the area

> All materials are durable

This coastal beach house is set on a hill overlooking the bay beneath and what better way to bathe than outside on the deck? It's a vacation home so all formality is set aside.

ESCAPE ARTISTRY

This award-winning vacation home is built on a breathtaking hillside setting, and is constructed from natural materials. The design's emphasis is on the pleasure of texture and color, and ease of living.

Architect Ken Crosson has conceived the home as one long rectangle that can be closed up when the family leave for their main urban home. To make this happen, everything had to be simple.

Ken Crosson believes that vacation homes should be an expression of a different lifestyle and social organization. They should have great connection to their environment.

"They are an opportunity to experiment and challenge conventions," he stated.

Crafted from unadorned wood, the bathroom area was kept minimal to make washing simple. Showers can be taken in the morning sunshine with the doors thrown open, and there is no need for a privacy screen because there are no close neighbors.

Above
Bathing while taking in the view from the wood deck is a unique experience by day, and at night there is a starry display.

Opposite
The spacious master bathroom features a large showerhead that pours down a powerful and relaxing waterfall.

The full-size tub on wheels can be filled inside and rolled out onto the front deck to take in the coastal vista or, if bathing at night, the starry sky.

Ken Crosson's design for the bathroom was inspired by his experience of farm life. Slatted wood floors were designed to imitate the removable gratings found in sheepshearing sheds. A stainless steel tray located below the slatted wood collects the water to drain it.

All of the fittings are raised from the floor level, making them easy to maintain. In amongst this simplicity, there is one

Above

A single mixer faucet and a sink provide basic but chic bathing facilities.

Right

The framed tub on rubber wheels is full-size, and can be filled from the faucet mounted on the wall.

extravagance, and that's a towel warmer. A touch of urban life somehow sneaked in to the design.

The walls in the master bathroom are lined with clear-finished plywood, as is the ceiling, giving an overall gentle honey glow to the room. The plywood is also easy to maintain. Wiping it down after a shower is good housekeeping practice but who does that on vacation? So, a wipe-down once a week is sufficient to keep it looking good.

Another thoughtful aspect of the bathroom design is that anyone coming up from the beach can walk straight into the shower area without bringing sand inside the remainder of the house. The Stockholm showerhead is large enough to rain down water to wash any grains of sand through the slatted wood floor.

Ken Crosson adds he had a desire to create a vacation experience as close to camping as possible. "It was all about getting back to nature and living at a slower pace."

He achieved his dream and during the process successfully challenged a few conventions that will benefit us all.

DESIGN SUMMARY

▶ Clear-finished plywood interior walls and ceilings for consistency of material

▶ Full-size tub can be rolled outside

▶ Large shower head for a full water flow

▶ Simple, clean architectural lines

▶ No-fuss maintenance

Right

A dramatic integrated sink was created from a slab of honey-gold limestone from Portugal.

Below

Slide to turn on this faucet design.

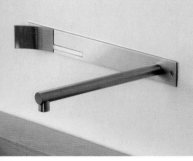

The inspiration for this ultra-modern minimalist bathroom in the Hollywood hills was to merge inside and outside by using stunning barrier-free design that makes the most of the view beyond.

WINDOW ON THE WORLD

Left
The egg-shaped
bathtub is made
of honey-gold
polished
limestone,
and was
designed for the
space. Huge
windows give
bathers a
wonderful view
of the hill beyond.

Above

A sandblasted glass door filters light into the bedroom beyond. Instead of a handle, it has a fingerhole in keeping with the uncluttered design.

Gerhard Heusch is one of the most distinguished architects working in America so it is not at all surprising that he had very definite views when it came to the refurbishment of his home in the Hollywood hills. He and fellow architect David Wick at Heusch, Inc. worked on a scheme that would open each room in the home to the natural world beyond, giving uninterrupted views to the horizon without loss of privacy.

Above + below

The bath is filled by a simple
Italian-designed mixer faucet
with a satin matte finish. The
wall-mounted box shelf is made
from Brazilian walnut.

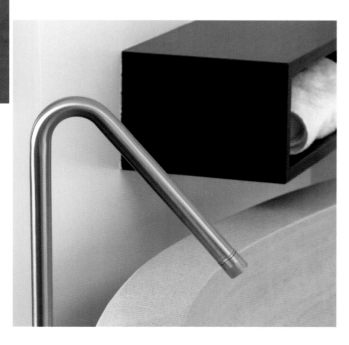

Stage one of the project involved raising the entire house 12 feet in the air to circumvent local building codes. As David Wick explained, this allowed the master bedroom and bathroom to face the rolling green hill rather than an ugly retaining wall, a strategy exactly in line with the owner Gerhard Heusch's desire to bring the outside inside.

Huge windows give floor-to-ceiling views and the mirror above the twin sinks is extended beyond the edge of the window frame, creating a clever optical illusion that there's nothing solid behind it, a trick that serves to further blur the division between the interior and exterior.

This is a spacious bathroom with no place for fussy detail. Taking center stage is a fabulously simple egg-shaped bathtub made from polished stone. The bathtub is an exquisite custom design manufactured in Portugal and then shipped to the U.S. The hue of the bathtub matches the hue of the honey-gold limestone integral countertop and sink. The same limestone was also used to line the walls of the walk-in shower stall.

The minimalist steel faucets are made by the same manufacturer and employ a sliding mechanism to start the flow of premixed water. These fittings have a matte finish that harmonizes with the subdued, natural feel of the bathroom.

Below the sink countertop is a sleek Italian-designed wall console made of Brazilian walnut. Cabinetry is used sparingly in this space, floating free of the floor, and is a core element in the overall design.

David Wick explained: "We wanted each piece to float above the ground, adding to the sense of the entire house floating above the landscape."

Above

Walnut flooring
merges into
limestone flooring
when it reaches
the shower area.

Minimalist design can seem chilly and uncomfortable, but an intriguing and unique mix of materials has avoided this pitfall. Brazilian walnut is also used for the flooring, adding rich tones that create a warm effect; it is is also the perfect partner for the superb honey-gold limestone that was used for the bathtub, the sleek countertops, and the smooth wall cladding in the shower stall. A solid door would be totally out of place in an area that was designed to be open and free from restriction, so David Wick designed a

DESIGN SUMMARY

▶ Glass blurs the barrier between exterior and interior

▶ Custom-design limestone bath

▶ Wall-hung cabinetry floats

▶ Walnut flooring

▶ Faucets use latest slide technology

Left
The shower valve has a single control lever for both the water flow and the temperature.

Above
The shower stalll is a simple walk-in design with a built-in bench.

Right
The unique modern showerhead provides a wide, refreshing spray of water.

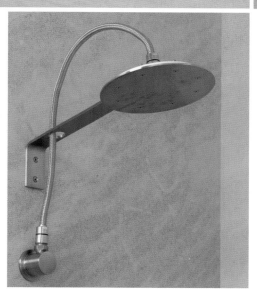

sandblasted glass door which, when it is closed, filters light into the bedroom beyond. A fingerhole replaces a conventional door handle, keeping the glass surface smooth and its line uncluttered.

The painted dry wall finish is seen throughout the dry area in the bathroom; its whiter shade of pale is very calming, providing a veil-like cover to the wall material.

Attention to detail and a determination to keep faith with the original design brief are the secrets of success in this elegant and minimal room.

Opposite
The cabinets in the dressing area are veneered with rift-cut American maple and finished with clear lacquer. The countertops are made of a dark green French limestone with a honed finish.

BEACH RETREAT

The owner of this beachside home asked Los Angeles architect Dean Nota for a master suite that would serve as a self-contained retreat, with a bathing room that could provide openness with seclusion. Here's how he interpreted the request.

Right
The Vola polished chrome faucet by Arne Jacobsen is in the design collection of the Museum of Modern Art in New York.

Above
Behind this opaque glass door is the toilet and more storage facilities.

Right

The view from the
dressing area
down to the
walk-in double
shower and steam
room suite.

Left

The smooth
countertop is the
perfect place for a
display of
architectual
decorative vases.

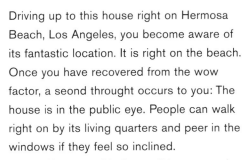

Driving up to this house right on Hermosa
Beach, Los Angeles, you become aware of
its fantastic location. It is right on the beach.
Once you have recovered from the wow
factor, a seond throught occurs to you: The
house is in the public eye. People can walk
right on by its living quarters and peer in the
windows if they feel so inclined.

However, this factor did not perturb
the owner because the home is in an ideal
location for him. As a successful
businessman, he leads a frenetic life. Being
at this beach location is handy because he

Opposite

One side of the double shower, showing the full effect of the sand-colored limestone, called Crema Europa. The tub faucet was designed by Philippe Starck.

Right

The windows, set high in the wall, can open and help to ventilate the steamy spa area. The tub is sunk into the green French honed limestone floor.

can reach the airport easily, fly out for a meeting, fly back, and be back in his home on the beach by sunset if he wants.

The home was originally a small beach shack, remodeled by architect Dean Nota in agreement with the owner. The ground floor level is public, the next level up is designed for more formal entertaining, and the top level is a private domain where the owner can unwind and entertain on an informal basis.

The site had some big issues to resolve: the adjacent buildings were close, the view was captivating, and the front of the house was a public area. The trick was to maintain a sense of privacy, yet allow the owner to stand in the steam room and still see the ocean view. The client required a spa-like space and gave Dean Nota a reference of a spa facility.

The plan of the master suite is conceived as a linear sequence of spaces leading from the sleeping room at the beach end, through the dressing area, and terminating in the bathing room.

The symmetrical arrangement of cabinetry and mirrors in the dressing area allows for uninterrupted contact with the ocean through a direct line of sight and reflected views. "It is an experiment in perception," explained Dean Nota, who spent some time talking to his client to ascertain what was important.

The axis of symmetry orders the arrangement of "his and her" sunken showers with the steam room and bath at the center for common access. The entire composition is contained under a gently curving roof with a large operable skylight over the bathing well. The owner can pop open the 8- by 4-foot skylight in clear weather, sit in the tub, and

Below
The tub is recessed flush with the limestone floor creating a platform at one end. This acts as somewhere to place candles or pampering oils, and towels ready for when you step out.

Above
Gentle gradient steps lead down to the double shower area at the back of the house.

look at the stars. A welcome end to any frantic day.

The walls on this bathing level are covered with 12-by-12-inch sand-colored limestone slabs called Crema Europa. Two exhaust fans and the windows help to ventilate the bathing area.

Walking up the few gentle steps to the dressing area with two sinks set into the curving cabinetry brings you closer to the panoramic sea view.

The zone here is all about getting dressed, regardless of whether you are distracted by the view, or by the wall-mounted television screen located opposite the bed, which is just at the end of the dressing zone. When not in use, the television slides back in

Above

Accessories such as this
wooden tub rack are made
of natural materials,
in keeping with the spa
ambience in this area.

DESIGN SUMMARY

▶ Sand-colored honed limestone walls
with green countertops and floor

▶ Bathtub is recessed into the floor

▶ Low-voltage ambient lighting

▶ Bathing area away from the public eye

▶ Windows can open for ventilation

▶ Entire area designed in zones

the custom-designed cabinetry, leaving the area media-free until the next time there's something worth watching.

Behind the cabinetry on one side of the area is a wardrobe with more of the custom-designed cabinetry. Toilet facilities are located on the opposite side of the zone.

The flooring in the dressing zone is 3-inch solid American maple with a clear matte finish, in keeping with the desire to retain a natural ambience. The selection of cream and green limestone in the bathing zone was intended to evoke a theme of sand and sea; in the dressing zone, the wood recalls a beachside boardwalk, refined for an interior. The use of different flooring surfaces helps to delineate the two zones.

Lighting throughout this informal living floor is recessed incandescent fittings mounted all over the ceiling. The bathing area features low-voltage fixtures made of stainless steel with glass lenses, designed by Bega specifically for a wet environment. The mirror lights are also a low-voltage type and feature elegant, modern Italian glass covers.

During the day much of the area is lit by natural light flooding through the skylight, and from windows at the beach end of the space. At night, the mood changes to an overall subtle light, with task fittings providing more light when necessary. Since both moon and candle light are the other two options here, it would be interesing to know how often the electric light is used.

WORKING WITH DESIGN PROFESSIONALS

Regardless of the scope of a project or the size of a budget, every homeowner will benefit from a consultation with a design professional. The reason is that few of us are trained to take a three-dimensional approach to the design of our surroundings.

We might know what we want, and what we like, but be less equipped to know the best way to turn that dream into reality. Even more important, design professionals are trained to see the potential of a project.

The challenge is to find a design expert that best suits the scale of your project. If your new bathroom involves major structural changes, a relocation of utilities, or an addition to your home, consider an architect with residential experience. If you plan to remodel within the existing footprint of your current bathroom without significant structural changes, hire a certified bathroom designer. In some cases, it may make sense to consult both types of experts: the architect on style, structural issues, and local codes; and the bathroom designer for expertise on cabinetry, materials, fixtures, and storage.

Begin the search by asking friends and homeowners in your area for their recommendations. You can also obtain the names of qualified individuals from national organizations that license and certify design professionals, such as The American Institute of Architects (www.aia.org) or The National Bathroom and Bath Association (www.nkba.com).

Interview several professionals before making a final decision. Look at work that reflects your home's architecture, or is similar to the style of bathroom you want to build.

During the initial consultation, show the professional sketches and photographs that convey your taste, style preference, and design ideas. Also, present a preliminary budget to help guide you toward viable options. At this stage, be prepared to discuss design fees. Is the person willing to negotiate a flat fee for the project, or do they charge an hourly rate? If they bill by the hour, check how much time they expect the project to take. Although design fees vary, estimate the professional's costs to be between 5 and 15 percent of the project's budget.

Do not hesitate to ask questions or to clarify information. Ask the person to walk you through the project from start to finish in order to understand the process. Review drawings and photographs of their previous projects and ask for references. Also ask if you can visit a completed project to evaluate their work before making a decision.

When you have done your homework, it is important to hear what the architect or bathroom designer has to say about your project. Listen to ideas with an open mind and do not be surprised if your vision of the bathroom evolves as you gather information. Professionals approach design from a different perspective than a homeowner; they may point out possibilities you had not considered, or based upon their experience, they may eliminate options. Always keep in mind that the objective is for the design professional to be guided by your vision and your goals, not the other way around. It is your home, your budget, and you are always in control of the project. If the person is not responding to your ideas, or is trying to impose their signature style on you, take that as a cue to move on to the next candidate; communication and a solid working relationship are crucial for success.

Once you have made a decision to hire, set a firm budget, and agreed on terms, your project will proceed to the design phase. The architect or bathroom designer will show you an initial set of plans for review and revision. If you require alterations, now is the time to make them. Even small changes to a final design can be costly and cause delays.

MANAGING THE CONSTRUCTION

While meticulous planning will minimize any problems arising during construction projects, they will not be eliminated entirely. From sorting out small issues, such as cleaning up the site daily, to dealing with more pressing matters, such as extended delays or quality of workmanship, the construction process is layered with details and complexities.

Most state governments have a list of organizations that govern contractors, issue licenses, and set specific standards of performance. To understand your rights as a consumer, contact the appropriate organization to familiarize yourself with the regulations before hiring a professional to work on your home. Then put a plan of work in place.

OTHER POINTS TO CONSIDER INCLUDE:

► Draw up a contract for signature that states the scope of the project, the estimated cost, a payment schedule, and a reasonable time frame for completion. Include details such as how the contractor plans to seal off the work zone, what time workers will arrive each morning, and that they will clean up the site daily.

► Read the fine print. Many standard contracts outline terms for settling disputes; some limit the homeowners' ability to take legal action. Make all of the changes before signing the agreement.

► Set up a portable file to organize project paperwork and include sections for payments, receipts, and notes of meetings or conversations with the contractor.

► Make a list of questions and/or concerns that arise as the construction progresses. Arrange a weekly meeting with the contractor to review the timetable and resolve issues.

► When construction is complete, conduct a walk-through to inspect cabinets, surfaces, appliances, lighting, outlets, and plumbing before signing off on the project.

► Compile a list of items that need to be addressed and withhold final payment until each matter has been resolved to your complete satisfaction.

INDEX

SOURCES

ARCHITECTS + DESIGNERS

Andrew Bannister
Design Republic
The Courtyard, Balaton Place
Snailwell Road, Newmarket
Suffolk CB8 7YP, U.K.
Tel + 1638-676-750
www.design-republic.net

Lou Ann Bauer, ASID
Bauer Interior Design
1286 Sanchez St
San Francisco, CA 94114
Tel + 415-282-2788
www.bauerdesign.com

Nick Berman Case Study
contact:
nickbermandesign.com and
bermanrosetti.com

Simon Carnachan, NZIA
Crosson Clarke Carnachan
P. O. Box 37521
Parnell, Auckland,
New Zealand
Tel + 64-9-309-4209
simon@ccca.co.nz

Leonardo Chalupowicz, AIA
Architect
3527 Landa St
Los Angeles, CA, 90039
Tel + 323-660-8261
www.chalupowicz.com

Ken Crosson, NZIA
Crosson Clarke Carnachan
15 Bath Street
Parnell, Auckland,
New Zealand
Tel + 64-9-302-0222

Timothy Geutzlaff
TMG + Associates
1232 Spring Street
Saint Helena, CA 94574
Tel + 707-963-9690
www.tmga.net

Heusch Inc.
David Wick
1251 N Clark Street
Los Angeles, CA 90069
Tel + 310-652-7707
www.heusch.com

Glen Irani, AIA
410 Sherman Canal
Venice, CA 90291
Tel + 310-305-8840
www.glenirani.com

Nestor Matthews
Matthews Studio
1099 23rd Street, *4
San Francisco 91107
Tel + 415-550-6700
www.matthewsstudio.com

Dean Nota Architect, AIA
2465 Myrtle Avenue
Hermosa Beach, CA 90254
Tel + 310-374-5535
www.nota.net

John J. Reed and Marisa
Solomon
Reed Architectural Group
1501 Colorado Avenue
Santa Monica, CA 90404
Tel + 310-393-9128
email: ragarch@cs.com

Bill Reichert,
J. P. Walters Design
Associates
4421 Park Boulevard,
Suite 201
San Diego, CA. 92116
Tel + 619-692-9655
www.jpwaltersdesign.com

PRODUCTS

Atelier Design Group
(Struch and Modero
products)
Tel + 973-762-2447
www.atelierdesigngroup.com

Atlas Pulls
Atlas Homewares
326 Mira Loma Avenue
Glendale, CA 91204
Tel + 818-240-3500
www.atlashomewares.com

Devon Stone Limited
7 Knowle Mews
Dalditch Lane
Budleigh Salterton,
Devon EX9 7AH, U.K.
Tel + 1395-446-841
www.devonstone.com

Fired Earth Interiors
3 Twyford Mill, Oxford Road
Adderbury, Nr BANBURY
Oxfordshire OX17 3SX, U.K.
Tel + 1295-812-088
www.firedearth.com
brochures@firedearth.com

Kohler
444 Highland Drive
Kohler, WI 53044
Customer Service:
Tel + 800-4-KOHLER
(800-456-4537)
or 920-457-4441
Literature:
Tel + 800-4-KOHLER
(800-456-4537)
www.us.kohler.com

Ann Sacks
8120 NE 33rd Drive
Portland, OR 97211
Customer Service:
tel + 800-278-8453
Tile: tel + 800-278-8453
Literature: tel + 800-278-TILE
(800-278-8453)
www.annsacks.com

Sonoma Cast Stone Corp
(Also Hoesch and THG
faucets)
133 Copeland Street
Petaluma, CA 94952
Tel + 707-283-1888
877-283-2400 (toll free)

PICTURE CREDITS

P1, LeFroy Brooks; p2, Architect Simon Carnachan's bathroom, photography by Patrick Reynolds; pp4/5, Burgh House hotel bathroom, photography by Andy Pini; pp8/9, photography by Jay Graham; pp10/11, 12/13, 14/15, photography by Douglas Hill; p17, Susan Ungar's beachside bathroom photographed by Claude Lapeyre; p19, Jay Graham; p21, Kohler USA; pg 22, Corian sink, vanity, and shelving unit; p24, Douglas Hill; pp25, 26, Jay Graham; p27, Brady Architectural Photography for J. P. Walters Design Associates; p28, Marion Brenner, design by Matthews Studio; p29, Jay Graham; pp30/31,32/33, Douglas Hill; p34, Claude Lapeyre, photographer, from *Collections on Display* (Sterling Publishing Co., Inc.); p35, Bauer Design; p36, Smith house bathroom designed by Simon Carnachan; p38, Fired Earth tub design; p39, private bathroom by Claude Lapeyre; p40, top, left, Fired Earth tile and tub; top right, Burgh House Hotel bathroom by Andy Pini; bottom left, Fired Earth sink; bottom right, Sonoma Cast Stone; p 41, Burgh House hotel bathroom by Andy Pini; pp42/43, mosaic tile photography by Andrew Bannister; pp44/45, Villeroy & Boch Subway tile design and fixtures; p46, Sonoma Cast Stone trough; p47, Corian integrated countertop and sink; p48, Douglas Hill; p50, top, Kohler USA, bottom, Devon Stone; pp51,52, Douglas Hill; p53, top left, Design Republic, & top right, Jay Graham;

pp54/55, J. P. Walters Design Associates; p56, top, Madero Box modular units, Atelier Design Group; p57, Madero unit through Atelier Design group; pp58/59, Douglas Hill; p60, detail of Villeroy & Boch Private Lounge Room design; p61, wall-hung Massai design vanity, Atelier Design Group; p62, Kohler USA; p63, top, mist-free mirror, & bottom, Atlas Homewares design; pp64/65, 66/67, Douglas Hill; p68, Villeroy & Boch Aveo design; p69, Douglas Hill; p70, Andy Pini; p71, KOS Italian-designed chromatherapy shower stall; p72, Philippe Starck Edition 1 tub; p72, top, Kohler USA, bottom, LeFroy Brooks shower fixture; p74, from left: Kohler undermount sink, Corian sink, Massai glass sink; p76, tub design by Fired Earth UK; p77, drop-in double-tub design by Lord Foster for Hoesch; p78, tub design by Corian; Aviva round tub design from the Hoesch Collection; p79, enclosed shower unit by Kohler USA; p80, Kohler toilet set; p81, Cygne faucet design from the French THG range; p81, wall-mounted faucet by Kohler USA.

Case Studies: P106–111, Surface Winner case study, photography by Max Spenser Morris with details by Neil Davis. All other case studies photographed by Douglas Hill.

ACKNOWLEDGMENTS

Lynn Bryan would like to thank Susan Breen for her initial vision of this book. Thanks also to Douglas Hill for the bathroom photographs, which were taken especially for this book. To Mary Staples, thanks, for once again designing with flair.

The BookMaker is also grateful to the following manufacturers: Dupont, Villeroy & Boch, Kohler USA, Sonoma Cast Stone, Devon Stone and Burgh Island House hotel in the UK, Fired Earth UK, Atlas Homewares, Atelier Design Group, USA, and LeFroy Brooks for their product information.

To all of the homeowners, architects, and interior designers who created such fantastic bathrooms, a sincere thank you. We could not have done this book without your talent. Thank you.